Master
the
Metaverse

Praise for
Big Things Have Small Beginnings
By Wes Berry

Wall Street Journal Bestseller
USA TODAY Bestseller
Barnes & Noble's Top 5 Best Sellers of All Books Worldwide
Amazon #1 Best Selling Author, #1 Hot New Release, and
International Best Seller
Business Insider, Books to Help You Build Wealth
and Get More Done
New York Book Festival, Winner Best Business Book

"Wes, I love your new book...I love everything about it! Keep up
the great work!"
Kevin O'Leary, star of *Shark Tank*

"Big Things Have Small Beginnings is the truest thing I've
heard! I'm all about it!"
Bethanne Frankel, CEO of *Skinnygirl*

"Congratulations on winning first place in the Southern
California Book Festival for 'Big Things have Small beginnings.'
Congratulations, Wes! Keep changing lives!"
Daymond John, CEO of FUBU

Master
the
Metaverse

BY BESTSELLING AUTHOR
WES BERRY

Always stay ahead. Always do your research.

Table of Contents

Part V — Implications of a Metaversal World

Introduction

The metaverse, or as some call it, "the new internet," is the next phase of the digital revolution. Technology has always played an important role in creating innovative industries and driving new economies. The metaverse is the newest revelation in the digital space that tech companies are racing to develop. It is a realm of virtual reality (VR) that will change the way we view and live in the physical world.

So what exactly is the metaverse? In short, it is a multi-dimensional space where people will have the ability to interact as avatars. This digital version of yourself will be able to gather with family and friends, work, shop, attend sporting events, and perform various other real-world activities in the digital world. Such an immersive experience will break down the barriers that presently divide us, allowing people to connect anywhere at any time.

To give you an idea of what the metaverse looks like, let us look at a few examples. *The Sims*, a video game launched in 2000,

created a virtual world where people controlled tiny digital avatars. In the game, players tell their avatar when to eat, sleep, and work. They also choose the types of interactions the avatars have with one another, ultimately emulating a life very similar to our own.

The immensely popular video game, *Fortnite*, has been described as a metaverse playground. *Fortnite* users are submerged into a virtual 3D space where non-gaming and gaming elements are combined. The game has given users a small taste of the kinds of events the metaverse will hold.

In April of 2020, *Fortnite* held a global in-game virtual concert that twenty-seven million players attended. Those in attendance were able to fly around a gigantic virtual version of Travis Scott while he performed for the event. There were also several mini-games available to entertain concert-goers who attended the show.[1]

If you have seen the *Matrix* movies, you have been exposed to a fully immersive metaverse experience. The humans in the film hooked themselves up to technology that transported them into a world created by artificial intelligence. They could perform actions in the virtual world that could not be done in the physical world.

Ready Player One is another instance of a virtual world being explored in film. People could build, demolish, make transactions, and live an entire alternate life within the digital space.

The metaverse uses both virtual and augmented reality (AR) in its technology. While virtual reality allows the user to interact with the world around them, augmented reality allows them to see the world as it is with an overlay of visual, audio, and other sensory input. As a result, the digital content appears to be in the same space as the user.

Google Lens is an example of augmented reality, powered by artificial intelligence. Take a picture of something unidentifiable, like a random plant, and the app will give you its name. Scan text in another language, and Google Lens will translate the words.

Need directions? The Live View in Google Maps will lay directions over the real world and guide you to your destination. Do you want to see how a new sofa will look in your living room? Use the AR technology in Google Search to snag a digital image and impose the object over your space.

There is no doubt that the global pandemic found many fitness buffs stuck in the house without access to exercise equipment. As

a result, the fitness industry took a major hit with all of the gym closings. So, it is not surprising that many fitness companies have adopted (AR) technology. They are creating headsets that give you access to celebrity trainers and more. You can play games like ping pong or train as a boxer with different apps while at home. The metaverse will push AR and VR technology to be an integral part of our daily lives.

The new realm will change content creation methods, virtual economies, and how we present ourselves in the world. Content creators can design worlds to offer their subscribers experiences they could not live out in the physical world, and these newly-formed communities can attend special events together.

The metaverse will be an extension of the real-world economy. Avatars will exchange cryptocurrencies and use them to purchase and invest in products and services. Non-fungible token (NFT) art will be on display in galleries, and visitors will experience the 3D pieces as the artists truly intended. For anyone who previously did not understand the value of NFTs, hopefully, the metaverse will provide a bit more clarity about how they will be used.

The fashion industry will also be transformed as the digital revolution takes place. Clothing brands are already setting up

virtual stores, with designers creating outfits from head to toe for avatars. Your digital representative will be able to change for work meetings, parties, fashion shows, and other social events. Of course, the metaverse stores accept cryptocurrency for payment, so users will have to make sure their digital wallets are not empty. It is clear that the metaverse will have its own economic system, with cryptocurrency being the chief transactional method.

Our corporate landscape will look completely different than it does now. The metaverse will greatly impact how people get to work and how they perform tasks. Just think of the metaverse as Zoom on steroids for company meetings. Your avatar will sit in conferences, seminars, and training sessions, next to coworkers in a setting that feels real with their presence.

How we shop and sample products will be affected. You will be able to sit at home and compare various brands and explore what they have to offer before conveniently ordering through your device. In-store experiences will be much more interactive. Imagine using AR to try on clothing and getting a full 360-degree view. Or use it to quickly guide you to the products you wish to purchase.

You can try on makeup or a different hair color before committing to the purchase. This is good news for consumers and companies alike. The customer is less likely to return the item and will spend more since they are confident in their purchase.

But where did the metaverse come from? Well, in the beginning, there was the internet. Born in 1991, the World Wide Web kick-started the exploration of possibilities for a digital world. The word itself was initially used in the 1992 novel *Snow Crash* by Neal Stephenson. This work of science fiction depicted a virtual world where people interacted as avatars with each other and artificial intelligent agents.

The 1990s continued to introduce concepts and upgrades in technology that improved the internet's security and ease of use. These enhancements continued as the new millennium rolled in and video games like *The Sims* and *Second Life* introduced virtual worlds to game players.

Then, in 2006, the *Roblox* platform came along, and users could create games and play games created by others. Communities were now forming, and people were interacting with each other online in a new way. As 2010 grew closer, cryptocurrency began to emerge in the form of Bitcoin. With Bitcoin came the blockchain,

which is a public ledger of all transactions. At the same time, video games continued to be influential in the metaverse's early days, and play-to-earn technology became popular. Then, another book came along in 2011, *Ready Player One*, and introduced a virtual world to a new generation.

In 2016, the video game *Pokémon Go* was the first to utilize AR technology to lay a virtual world on top of the real world. The following year, *Fortnite* launched a multi-player game that gave many the look and feel of the metaverse.

As the use of cryptocurrency grew, so did the use of decentralized apps. These are apps that are not under the control of a single organization. We will dive deeper into them later in the book, but the concept of no entity having authority to freeze your account and take away the accumulated items is essential to the metaverse.

In April of 2020, the first concert was held in the metaverse by Travis Scott and Marshmello. In October 2021, Facebook announced it would be rebranding to Meta. The technology to merge the physical and digital worlds is no longer off in the distant future. It is here now.1

This book will continue with an in-depth discussion of the metaverse's beginnings and the technologies and constructs contributing to its existence. We will talk about the innovative minds who had the vision early on and how their ideas have been implemented.

Facebook has big plans for the metaverse's future, which they have made public with the rebrand. But what exactly are they planning? This book will go over the various products and services the company plans to offer and how they will affect your day-to-day living. There is a slew of positive benefits to be gained from the use of such a powerful tool. Users will be able to experience just about any activity they desire, and the citizens of the world will connect in unimaginably creative ways.

The metaverse is not just being built by one giant conglomerate. It is a combination of different entities coming and chipping into this virtually augmented reality. Therefore, you can virtually hop into other worlds created by separate entities and use your money. All you need to do this is a crypto wallet. As long as you have your wallet authenticated, you will be able to use your crypto money anywhere in the metaverse.

The metaverse will look different depending on who is using it. For example, entrepreneurs, companies, and investors will each use the Metaverse differently. Let's take a comprehensive investigation into what the Metaverse will look like for these different end-users.

Is the Metaverse Inevitable?

In the real world, we have our universe and theoretically several other universes. Together, all of this is called the multiverse. Similarly, in the virtual world, we can see different universes being created by various apps, games, or simulations, and the whole thing is termed as the metaverse. Perhaps the multiverse theory could be fully realized through the development of the metaverse. In time, perhaps, the metaverse could evolve into what the science fiction series *Star Trek* demonstrates as a holodeck? After all, an awful lot of what was conceived in science fiction has been developed into everyday real life.

Let's get started.

> *Make no mistake; the metaverse will forever change the way we use the internet as we presently know it. What's to come is a revolution unlike anything we've ever seen.*

Chapter 1

THE NEW INTERNET

When most people think about the internet, they envision the mid-to late-nineties and all of the wonders the decade brought with it—at least, that's typically the way it is for those who were alive to witness the birth of the internet. Those born into it can't quite fathom just how amazing it was to see the internet come to life. Fast-forward to 2022, and today's generation will likely feel the same way over the birth of the metaverse. Indeed, the metaverse is a completely new take on the internet—the internet on steroids, if you will. If the concept of the metaverse is new to you, you're not alone. While we've seen glimpses of what it can be, we have yet to fully understand the metaverse's might.

Some people associate the metaverse with "stepping into" the internet. If you've ever experienced virtual reality (VR), you have a basic understanding of what the metaverse will be like. But up until recently, virtual reality was limited to rather basic interpretations of actual reality. All that's changed, of course, as today's virtual worlds rival what you see in movies—even real life. Where the metaverse aims to change virtual worlds forever is with its merging of the internet.

Make no mistake; the metaverse *will* forever change the way we use the internet as we presently know it. What's to come is a revolution unlike anything we've ever seen. And while there have been *improvements* on the internet over the years—faster connection times, better content, and more ways to stay connected—the metaverse is the first major advancement to come along since the internet's inception. And really, the metaverse is all about connectivity at its core. But it's *how* it connects people that has everyone talking. And because of this, human beings are about to embark on a journey that makes the most of nearly every modern-day innovation. Where we go from here is something that no one fully understands or realizes.

It's been clear from the outset that the metaverse's potential is limitless. And that potential will vary depending on the user. Some may wish to use the metaverse to hang out with friends or hold board meetings. Others may use it to perform trial runs on complex surgeries. And even still, some users may use the metaverse primarily to play video games. It's this broad range of possibilities that makes the metaverse so exciting. There will undoubtedly be a unique mix of users on the metaverse, each with their own objective for how they wish to make use of the new world. And that's one of the best aspects of the metaverse: its users aren't tied to any one activity or purpose. It's your world to do as you please, so if you want to use it sparingly to learn a few new things, that's perfectly fine.1

Realistically, though, it's a safe bet that once users get plugged in, the metaverse will take over much of their free time, just as the internet has done for the last 20+ years. Parents, in particular, can expect to implement rules of engagement, setting time limits and other boundaries to ensure their children get a healthy balance of real-world living. That said, the metaverse is poised to establish an unprecedented reality. While it shares many similarities and principles of the internet, the metaverse is capable of doing so much more, leading many to believe that it will become the normal way of life for its users.

And speaking of users, there's no doubt that the younger generation will find the metaverse to be much more accessible from the start. As for those who are old enough to remember when the internet came into existence, the metaverse may prove to be a challenging affair that requires plenty of time and patience to master, much like our elders whom we tried teaching video games, the internet, or smartphones to all those years ago.

The metaverse is the new internet, and it's going to revolutionize life as we know it. But how will all of this be possible? Won't we

> *The metaverse is the new internet, and it's going to revolutionize life as we know it.*

need new technology to harness the power of the metaverse and make use of its many wonders? Indeed, we will. Just like every other computer or video game console that's come out in the past, you need specific technology to take advantage of the newest toy. So, before we jump into the core components that make up the metaverse, let's examine some of the things you'll need to make it work in your home. If you don't understand some of the lingo discussed below, don't worry. We'll be getting into all of that later.

Running the Metaverse:
A Brief Rundown of What You'll Need

The metaverse is a digital universe that blends the virtual world with the real world. We're going to go on this journey together in much greater detail later in the book. But to give you a sneak peek, the metaverse is a virtual world where you can buy things, meet new people, work, learn, participate in games, and so much more.

Due to all of the groundbreaking things you can do in the metaverse, there is no shortage of technology in development for this virtual world. And believe when you hear—you're going to need cutting-edge technology if you want to be a part of this new reality.

It's not like in the old days when you could buy a Nintendo Entertainment System or even a more modern PlayStation 4 and simply plug it into your TV. Those days may be disappearing sooner than we think. If you decide that you want to step into the metaverse, you're going to need hardware. Fortunately, you don't *have* to spend a lot of money on high-tech gear. The prices for the tech that the metaverse calls for have gone down considerably in recent years, and that is perhaps by design. The ultimate goal of the metaverse and its creators is to get as many people plugged into it as humanly possible. If visions of the Matrix come to mind, you're not far off (more on that later).

For starters, you can use your smartphone to access a metaverse. But there is one glaring caveat that you should be aware of, and that is the fact that you will be missing the core experience of the metaverse. If you're just using a smartphone, you will miss out on the immersive experience that serves as one of the key driving forces behind the metaverse. We had a very brief discussion on virtual reality at the start of this chapter, but that is, in fact, one of the core components that makes the metaverse what it is: a virtual world with seemingly endless possibilities. That's not something you can get from a smartphone alone.

So, if you want the full, immersive experience, you must invest in a VR headset. There is another technology available for accessing the metaverse that's a bit more affordable, but we'll discuss that shortly. For now, let's assume you want to invest in the complete metaverse experience. Now, you might be thinking that you can run to your local big-box store and pick up the cheapest VR headset and jump into the metaverse. Well, not so fast. A VR headset will indeed help to immerse you in the metaverse, giving you a feeling of being present in its computer-generated world. But a headset of lower quality doesn't provide the immersiveness of a high-end unit. To help put this into better perspective, it's like buying a computer game.

While the game might run on most computers, it's going to look leagues better on a system that boasts a powerful graphics card and speedy processor. If you're not into computer games, the most basic example would be if you were to buy a Blu-Ray movie, only to bring it home and watch it on a small black-and-white television. Next to a bleeding-edge 4K TV, there's no comparison. So, to get the most enjoyment from the metaverse, you want a high-quality VR headset.

To date, it's been announced that VR headsets like the HTC Vive, Oculus Quest, Oculus Rift, PlayStation VR, Lenovo Mirage Solo, and Samsung HMD Odyssey will work with the yet-to-be-released metaverse. What's more, these VR systems aren't exactly cheap. You can expect to spend an average of $500 if you wish to own one of these headsets. But like all other forms of hot tech, you can also expect prices to drop as they become more mainstream. The Oculus Quest 2 stands tall as the most popular VR headset on the market. And there are less expensive options. We'll discuss this, along with the software you need, in greater detail in Chapter 9.

Once you are set up with a VR headset and the correct software, you can do amazing things, such as attend concerts, comedy, and sporting events from the front row, and enjoy NBA games in virtual reality. You can also experience horror, survival, fighting, and other complex emotions in first-person video gaming. For the working person, you can purchase business software and meet with people in boardrooms around the world. There will also be software that encourages you to exercise more, with VR that allows you to experience the thrill of mountain climbing, or ride through scenic winding roads in the Alps on your bike.

A wide variety of machine perception and AI capabilities allow you to create real voice, interaction, and mixed reality experiences that seamlessly combine virtual content with the user's actual world. These tools include *Passthrough* and *Spatial Anchors*. They also provide Scene Understanding tools that allow you to create complex experiences in your home spaces. These apps will soon be available in the Oculus Store as well as App Lab. You'll soon be able to see better scenes, a particular topic, or part of your professional world using virtual objects. There will be specialized controllers for hands—the idea is to feel like you are holding an object. You can feel its texture using the Interaction SDK. This will provide high-quality manual interactions as well as a library with touch gestures. Voice SDK also allows you to add voices.

Now, before you think that the metaverse will be "just another fad" that isn't worth spending your hard-earned money on, consider this: Meta, Facebook's new parent company, recently announced that they would be spending a staggering $10 billion to build on and improve the metaverse to get it where they want it. Let that figure sink in. *Ten billion dollars.* Even $10 million would be impressive. But when you start talking billions, there's some serious infrastructure taking place behind the scenes that would likely stump even the brightest MIT graduate. 2

So right out of the gate, the metaverse will have plenty to see and do.

Another Dimension?

So far, we've established that the metaverse is a new take on the internet. But what exactly does that mean? To answer that question, we need to take a few steps back and discuss precisely how the metaverse operates. Collectively, society understands the internet as a collection of texts, sounds, images, and videos on a computer or smartphone screen. Through the use of hardware, software, cables, and wireless technology, information is shared between users to form a giant digital "web."

> *It's in this new reality that you will be able to do things not possible in the real world.*

And because of the connectivity aspect of the internet, anyone can access this web of information as long as they have the right tools and equipment. The metaverse isn't unlike the current internet in this regard. Once you have these metaverse-specific tools and equipment you can access the metaverse and join in with other metaverse users. But once you're "in," that's where things are vastly different from the internet as we currently know it. The metaverse is truly another dimension—one that has the ability to take users to distant worlds and change our very perception of reality.

And it's in this new reality that you will be able to do things not possible in the real world. For example, the metaverse will let you instantly beam yourself or appear before your colleagues in a virtual boardroom or sit with your classmates at school—but without ever leaving your home. And it's this new dimension that will provide for humans in a way that hasn't been possible until now. How you navigate the metaverse won't necessarily be the same from day to day. In fact, it's unlikely to remain the same from hour to hour. Because the metaverse allows you to beam yourself wherever you want (within the metaverse, of course) in the blink of an eye, you get to choose what kind of experience you have in the metaverse.

Whereas computers, televisions, smartphones, and tablets display different worlds in a largely 2D manner, the metaverse immerses you in those worlds via the third dimension. And it's there that the metaverse emulates the real world (and the not-so-real world) for you to explore. Thanks to 3D technology, the metaverse can take you to far-off worlds or just a couple of blocks over. Truly, the diverse potential of the metaverse is a groundbreaking affair that holds wonders not yet dreamed of. Our limited understanding of this new virtual dimension is certain to expand as we grow accustomed to it. But for now, we'll have to wait for the metaverse to take on a life of its own, much like the internet has since it first came into existence.

There is little doubt that the engineers, scientists, and programmers who initially invented the internet could have possibly imagined that it would grow into the beast it is today. What started out as a revolutionary way to share data from one computer to another eventually morphed into a network for streaming movies, playing multi-player video games, meeting people, finding dates, buying and selling goods and services, and so much more. 3

It's not a stretch to say that the modern-day internet is an ever-growing invention of its users. New ideas come to the forefront, and those that stick end up changing the way we use the internet. The same is going to be true for the metaverse. Whatever early notions we have of this dimension are certain to change and evolve over time. But there first needs to be a vast collection of users from different societies using the platform for new innovations to come along and alter its course.

And users in the metaverse will certainly have an impact. At present, the internet is home to over 4.6 billion active users. That is nearly 60% of the Earth's total population. Interestingly, that figure is virtually identical to the number of people that use social media. As discussed, the metaverse is all about connectivity. As it so happens, that's what social media is all about, too. If this user base migrates to the metaverse, the platform will effectively have all of the internet using its services. That, in itself, is a huge success. So you can imagine the opportunities that await those who take part in it. We're certain to see new jobs come to the forefront of the metaverse; jobs that weren't possible before this new reality came along. The metaverse's users are going to meet new people in ways that weren't possible before its advent. 4

And if the metaverse has even a fraction of the impact on society than the internet did back in its heyday (and it will), it's safe to predict that the metaverse will quickly serve as home to a majority of the world's population. A scary thought, to be sure. But one that is rife with possibilities. It's going to take the innovative minds of today to tap into the metaverse and pull out amazing new possibilities that have yet to be imagined.

Conclusion

The internet has proven to be much more than we could have possibly imagined during its initial stages of life. Over time, it's grown and transformed as a result of the many people who use it on a daily basis. And it's safe to say that it will continue to change as time goes on. Of course, logic dictates that the same is likely to be true for the metaverse. But it's going to take time for metaverse users to have an impact on the platform.

Right now, we have a limited perception of what the metaverse will really be like, much like we did when the internet was first introduced. There will need to be societal influence from all over the world to shape the metaverse. But if we want it to reach its true potential, it's important not to make the same mistakes that have been made with the internet.

To ensure this, we first need to learn more about the metaverse. We know it's going to be a different reality that offers an alternative to many modern-day activities. Let's look at it in more depth.

Chapter 2

WHAT IS THE METAVERSE?

Mark Zuckerberg, one of the wealthiest men on the planet through his company Meta, is one of the metaverse pioneers. Having become the first self-made billionaire by the age of just 23 as a founder of Facebook, Mr. Zuckerberg appeared to be destined for greatness. And if the metaverse is any indication, he's well on his way to fulfilling that destiny. As if Facebook wasn't enough, perhaps Zuckerberg wanted to leave a legacy that he was solely responsible for. After all, no fewer than five people are credited as the creators of Facebook. 1

To be fair, Zuckerberg's vision of the metaverse is one built on Facebook's back. According to Zuckerberg himself, he wanted to take Facebook in a completely new direction; a direction that provided a new way for people to connect with one another and one that appeared to be ripped from the sci-fi realm itself. We get a better understanding of the metaverse and how it functions by looking deeper into its development.

When Zuckerberg began his quest (conquest?) to revolutionize the internet, he divided his Facebook staff into groups. Each group had a primary objective that they would focus on toward building the metaverse: virtual reality, communities, commerce, and creators. The divided staff researched various products to gain a better understanding of how they could fit into the metaverse mold. But the endgame for all of this research remained the same: to bring the metaverse to life. 2

It would appear that it was a success, so much so that Facebook officially underwent a name change to simply "Meta." The Facebook social media platform will stay the same for the foreseeable future, but the parent company that was formerly known as Facebook is now Meta. On that front alone, it's evident that Zuckerberg has big visions for his creation. An official worldwide launch of Meta's vision of the metaverse is still in the works, but there have already been rumblings from Meta that give a glimpse of what's to come. While there is still certainly much to do, we can see the metaverse world slowly taking shape from the small steps that have been made since its announcement in 2021.

In December of 2021, Meta released *Horizon Worlds* to the public. This application works with Quest 2 Virtual Reality (VR) headsets and lets users explore a large-scale 3D world, where they can interact with other users to see what the metaverse might be like. And make no mistake, the Quest 2 VR system will play a pivotal role in bringing the metaverse to life, as we've already discussed. Mark Zuckerberg proved to the world that he has high hopes for Quest VR systems, as the company formerly known as Facebook purchased Quest's parent company, Oculus, for $2 billion in 2014.

When Zuckerberg announced the metaverse, he did so as if it would be the true defining platform of his company. And it certainly doesn't appear that he's too off-base with that allusion. This platform is designed to make you feel like you're physically present in a virtual ecosystem, all while connecting with the many avatars of live users. The metaverse is currently under construction, and it will likely remain that way throughout its existence. But even in its infancy, we're already seeing features that make use of its incredible technology.

Virtual Reality Meets Actual Reality

Virtual Reality's (VR) promise has been looming large in the computing world for the past quarter-century, but it's only now becoming a reality for everyday people. As a refresher, VR is an interactive, 360-degree computer-generated simulation that mimics an environment. What this really means is you can interact with objects and environments on a screen as if they're really there.

This could be anything from being on stage at a concert to exploring an alien world. The possibilities are indeed pretty limitless. Also, because the action happens on screen, you don't have to worry about someone else getting in your space. Virtual reality is the secret ingredient that makes the metaverse possible. It's with this technology that developers will be able to provide a new realm for users to explore and build upon.

The main idea of VR is to allow people to share things with each other via the internet and the web. Imagine if you could share more than just a photo and a link to a web page. What if, instead of sharing your wedding photos with your Facebook friends, you could make it possible for others to view your wedding in virtual reality and continue attending the event in perpetuity? Imagine if historical events could be recorded in a way that allows people to relive them forever! These are the kinds of collaborative, social, virtual reality sharing that Meta might be exploring right now. The future of virtual reality is bright for sure, if that happens.

Although VR technology is used in a variety of fields, including medicine, science, and architecture, mainstream adoption is still very rare. VR is not being used as often as computers, smartphones, or even the internet. Oculus VR has rekindled interest in the field and looked for a while like it would revolutionize everything.

And ever since his purchase of Oculus, Zuckerberg has been working behind the scenes to figure out the best way to incorporate his vision of the metaverse into Quest VR systems. As with the initial beginnings of the internet and the people who brought up computers to access it, the same is sure to be true for the metaverse and VR headsets. Right now, options are limited when it comes to viable VR systems. There are only a handful that handles the technology well enough to run the metaverse, but there will undoubtedly be an onslaught of companies hopping aboard the metaverse train to cash in on the new realm full of possibilities. Meta is the clear leader in giving rise to bringing the metaverse to market. However, others such as Microsoft, are also developing their own renditions of what they see as the future of the metaverse. The idea of a multiverse of metaverses seems most likely.

Once the metaverse officially goes online and you have a suitable VR headset, you will be able to take advantage of the new worlds built to educate, entertain, and even employ. This wouldn't have been possible only a few years ago. Virtual reality has come a long way in recent years, and much of that success can be attributed to Oculus and its Quest VR systems. If you've only seen pictures or videos from early VR technology, you're going to be in for a shock. Today's VR technology and the systems that house it are capable of immersing you in worlds that emulate our own. The graphical innovations alone are enough to make most gamers drool, but it's the handling of 3D that really deserves praise.

Virtual Reality

We need to be able to clearly define VR if we are to understand why virtual reality is different from books, movies, paintings, or pieces of music. It is an interactive 3D computer-created virtual world that you can explore to make you feel like you are *there*. With virtual reality, you have the ability to experience things via your computer, even though they don't exist. If you take a look at a painting, you can experience the sights and sounds of Italy in the same way it was 250 years ago—that's the power of virtual reality. If you close your eyes and listen to classical or ambient music and begin dreaming about the world, that's a form of virtual reality. How about letting yourself get lost in a good book? That's certainly a form of virtual reality. The same holds true for movies and TV shows.

When you turn your head in any direction, including up and down, the 3D VR world turns with you. And because the graphical effects are so life-like, you really feel like you're in the imaginary world presented to you. Systems like the Quest 2 use unique proprietary controllers that allow you to pick up items and manipulate them in real-time. As the next step in immersive entertainment, you can expect to tap into VR's power. With the most recent advancements of VR, combined with high-speed internet and streaming, the metaverse now has the technology it needs to come to life. 3

But there are key components to virtual reality that make it what it is. For starters, it has to be believable—to feel as though you are in your virtual world on Mars or anywhere else, and if you fail to believe that belief, the illusion will vanish. It also needs to be interactive. The VR world must move along with you as you move. It's possible to watch 3D movies and be taken to another world. But it is not interactive.

Computer-generated graphics are also of prime importance. Why? Only powerful computers with realistic 3D computer graphics can create believable, interactive worlds that move in real-time as we move about them. Another essential ingredient is that you must be able to explore it. A VR world must be large and well-designed. No matter how realistic a painting may be, it only shows one scene from one viewpoint. Although a book may describe a complex virtual world, you can only explore it linearly as described by the author. But with 3D-VR, you can walk through the world and explore it first-hand.

And finally, the last piece of the VR puzzle is that it has to be immersive. VR must engage your mind and body to make it believable. Although paintings by war artists may give glimpses into conflict, they cannot convey the sound and feeling of battle. It's possible to play a flight simulator on your computer and lose yourself in an interactive, realistic experience that will last hours. The landscape will constantly change as your plane moves through it. However, it is not the same as a real flight simulator, where you can sit in a hydraulically controlled mockup of a real cockpit and feel real forces as it tilts and tips.

This is why we can't, on our computer screens, view a movie, read a book, listen to a classical orchestra, or look at a painting as virtual reality. They all offer partial glimpses into another reality, but they are not interactive, you can't explore them, and they're not entirely believable. You'll be able to see the planet Mars from a movie theatre screen and then remember that you are actually on Earth. The illusion will disappear if you notice something else in the room that interests you. These forms of entertainment are passive. They don't engage you in any way, no matter how plausible. VR is quite different. You feel like you're actually *there*. It's two-way interactive, as well. As you respond to what is shown, what you see and hear changes.

Moreover, there are different types of VR that must be considered. Virtual reality has been used as a buzzword to describe and market interactive video games, 3D movies, and TV shows. However, these are not VR, as they don't fully immerse the user in a virtual world. You can search for VR in your mobile app store and find hundreds of hits, even though a small cell phone screen cannot produce the immersive experience of VR. Interactive games and computer simulations only meet part of the definition above. There are many ways to create virtual worlds, and there is more than one way to do it. Let's explore them.

The first is the non-immersive type. If a highly realistic flight simulator is used on a PC at home, it might be considered non-immersive virtual reality. Some people don't want to or need to immerse themselves in another reality. A 3D model of a building might be created by an architect to show clients. It can be accessed on a computer with a mouse. Even though it may not immerse you fully, most people would consider that virtual reality. Computer archaeologists can also create 3D reconstructions of long-lost settlements that are interactive and easy to explore. Although they don't transport you back hundreds of years or recreate the sounds, smells, and tastes of prehistory or take you back to ancient times, they offer a richer experience than any pastel drawing or animated movie.

Next up, there is immersive VR, the type that the metaverse is counting on to bring Zuckerberg's plan to fruition. A computer model, or simulation, is required to create a realistic, richly detailed virtual world. This allows us to see and hear what we is in front of us, just like in real life.

A third component is hardware that can be linked to the computer and allows us to fully immerse ourselves in the virtual world while we move around. You would typically need to wear a head-mounted display, or HMD, with stereo sound and two screens. Alternately, we could use surround sound loudspeakers to project changing images from the outside.

To this day, VR stands as one the most popular technologies we've seen in a long time to grow as quickly as it has. And for a moment, the world waited with bated breath to see what kind of wonders awaited us. However, it was introduced around the same time that the internet was introduced. And we all know the interest we took in *that*. As a result, the appeal of VR slowly died off, as did its development. Although computer scientists had developed a method to create a web-based virtual world, the web itself was what most people were interested in. For the first time since television and video games, we were able to access reality in new ways. The internet let us search for information without the need for a dictionary or encyclopedia, we could shop online for the first time, and share our ideas, thoughts, and experiences via social media.

It was a truly groundbreaking innovation. And it had to be to take the focus off of virtual reality. It's true that we've seen some pretty cool things come out in the past several years that made great use of virtual reality. But we can all thank Mark Zuckerberg for bridging the gap between it and social media. Although VR is absolutely an essential component to the metaverse, Zuckerberg knew he needed something more to tie the metaverse and its use of advanced technologies together.

An Augmented Future

Augmented Reality (AR) is the final component to making the metaverse come to full life, and without it, the metaverse wouldn't be the metaverse. Like VR, AR has been around for a while, but it's becoming more and more popular as companies find new ways to integrate this technology into our everyday lives. So what is augmented reality? Basically, it is a technologically-powered overlay of digital content in the real world. Moreover, augmented reality increases awareness and understanding of the physical environment we live in by adding information about objects or events not visible to the human eye. It can be used in many different ways, from gaming and entertainment to education and social interaction. Augmented Reality brings both the digital world and the real world together in a way not possible with VR alone. But the two technologies need one another to function at their very best. 4

You may have even used early versions of AR on your smartphone or Nintendo 3DS game system. By using the camera built into such devices, the augmented reality technology presents digital imagery as an overlay of the real world around you. On its own, augmented reality has a lot of potential benefits. For one, it is projected to have a significant impact on the way we learn. AR will revolutionize the classroom by enabling students to interact with virtual objects that are in front of them while also being able to see their classmates. What's more, AR has the power to transform shopping experiences by allowing customers to view new products in context with their physical environment. It can also be used for entertainment purposes, such as bringing animated characters into the real world so kids can play with them.

Smartphones and tablets have made supercomputer power available to us all. When we travel, we don't want virtual reality; we want to experience the wonders around us in all their glory. What we really want is an *enhanced version* of the world around us. This is where AR enters the fray. AR is a way to enhance your real-life experiences. With AR, you can direct your smartphone camera toward a landmark or object, and relevant information will automatically pop up on your phone's screen. Whether it's simple text designed to provide you with more information or an overlay of additional objects and imagery, augmented reality connects users in the real world with the endless databases of information we have created together on the internet. Now we can navigate and explore the internet's ever-expanding data in an entirely new way. This is made possible by harnessing virtual reality and injecting it with the invaluable information found on the internet, thus giving birth to augmented reality. It adds a whole new layer of immersiveness that wasn't readily available with VR alone.

Let's put this into perspective. Imagine walking through your neighborhood park with a Meta headset on. You can clearly see what's in front of you and all around you. You can turn around and see directly behind you in real-time. But suddenly, a giant monster appears, charging directly in your path. It looks real; it even *sounds* real. Your controllers rumble with each step it takes. Using your controllers, you unsheathe a giant sword and slash the monster to pieces right before your very eyes. That's AR in action.

And while this certainly sounds cool—and it is—it's clear that AR does more than just enhance or improve the user experience. The technology is able to offer something on so many different levels, from education to consumerism to medical breakthroughs. So it's telling that early developers have chosen to implement this technology into the core of the metaverse experience. Without it, users would still feel tethered to reality in a way that the metaverse hopes to eliminate. And given the current state of the world, many people could use a break from reality. The metaverse is that break, assuming everything goes off without a hitch. But given the masterminds at work on the metaverse, it's unlikely that we'll see anything but a successful launch.

Conclusion

Mark Zuckerberg was instrumental in altering the course of the internet when he created Facebook. And with the impending launch of Meta's vision of the metaverse, he's poised to do it yet again. This time, however, the effect that his creation will have on everyday life is infinitely more profound in every way. The metaverse is truly its own unique reality, and it's shaping up to be a world that many people may prefer to stay in.

Given how many people have gravitated to social media and implemented it into their daily lives, it's only natural for the metaverse to have an equal amount of appeal, at minimum. The more probable outcome is a society of users who prefer the metaverse to reality. The marrying of VR and AR has cemented the metaverse as being a tangible world of wonders. So why would anyone want to leave it?

Many of the reported wonders of the metaverse can be traced back to other forms of media, such as movies and TV shows. It's therefore important to look into the history of certain works to gain an understanding of where we're headed. What was once deemed science fiction is now on the brink of a worldwide release.

Chapter 3

MONEY IN THE METAVERSE

Cash, credit cards, and debit cards are slowly becoming a thing of the past now. Given the uber styling of the metaverse, the fast-tracked monetary system provides another feather to its hat.

When you think of the metaverse, you might think of the virtual world-hopping, facilitated by the interconnection of zillions of web surfers. You're predominantly right to think so, but the one thing that provides the 'verse with all its potential power is the cryptic side of it: the blockchain.

Let's try and understand this evolution of the virtual industry. Initially, Web 1.0 was the super portal for connected systems and servers that you could use to search and explore the web. A centralized company's platform facilitated all this. Examples of these working mechanisms can be Google, Yahoo, and Microsoft.

Soon came in Web 2.0. It featured blogging, social connection sites, and monetization of users' data to facilitate the 'free' social media platforms like Facebook, Twitter, Snapchat, and TikTok.

Now, here comes the big thing, Web 3.0, which makes up the building blocks of the metaverse. It provides a decentralized economy of player-owned crypto assets and data and is supported by the advanced blockchain technology.

Terms like blockchain, decentralized, and crypto assets might make you feel very alienated and out of bounds. Don't worry. This chapter will make you feel at ease with these mainstays of the metaverse.

That being said, let's get into the details of how money works in the metaverse, where crypto is paramount and user convenience is maximized.

Let's get started.

Crypto Is King

Before diving into how Crypto is the ultimate facilitator of all the economic transactions in the metaverse, we need to understand how it works. As discussed earlier, the whole system works on the blockchain application. So, let's try and understand what this technology actually is.

Blockchain refers to a technology that permanently records all transactions in a decentralized database that is for everyone to see. This database is termed the ledger. We can understand this mechanism with the help of the most famous blockchain-powered cryptocurrency—Bitcoin. Every time you purchase 'X' quantity of Bitcoin, the transaction is recorded in the Bitcoin blockchain. This means that the record of your transaction has been made public to thousands of computers worldwide.

The fact that distinguishes this decentralized system from the one found in our conventional financial setup is that it is very difficult to rig or control. All the transactions are transparent and are out there for everyone to see. This is in stark contrast with our current banking system, which is highly centralized and non-transparent.

Another feature that makes cryptocurrency different from other forms of exchange is smart contracts. These are blockchain-based software routines that execute automatically when certain conditions are met. Ethereum is one of the most well-known tokens that uses this technology.

Let's take an example to explain this point further. Suppose that you wish to buy a digital object, like a piece of art or music. Now, you can use one of these smart contracts on the blockchain to determine your ownership of that particular piece. Once this is done, no one else can claim ownership of that specific object in the virtual space. Such digital things that you can own by following this procedure are called crypto assets.

The transactions in the metaverse take place on a one-to-one basis because of this advanced mechanism. There is no need for a third party or bank escrow to monitor the exchange. For example, if you wish to buy a digital asset worth $1 Million, you can agree to the smart contract, and the ownership will be directly transferred to you unless there is a dispute between the two parties.

The metaverse is not just being built by one giant conglomerate. It is a combination of different entities coming and chipping into this virtually augmented reality. Therefore, you can virtually hop into other worlds created by separate entities and use your money.

All you need in order to do this is a crypto wallet. As long as you have your wallet authenticated, you will be able to use your crypto money anywhere in the metaverse.

Crypto Wallet and its Uses

A crypto wallet is just like the actual wallet you carry every day. The only difference is that it will carry your crypto coins in place of carrying cash. You can use this virtual currency anywhere in the metaverse. In addition, the crypto wallet also holds your digital goods, your avatar's costumes, accessories, weapons, and decorations.

Now, here comes the fun part. You can use your wallet to purchase digital products like movies, music, and cool skins for your avatar. Not just this, you can also shop for physical world items. You can view '3D' models of the item you're shopping for and make a more informed decision.

The metaverse is also planning to connect these wallets with associate scores in the near future. These scores will gauge the permission you have for organizing public place broadcasts and interacting with people outside your social network.

If you act unethically in the 'verse, it could directly affect your associate score. This development can incentivize users to behave well inside the virtual world.

Help Yourself (Shopping in the Metaverse)

Gone are the days of standing in lines of physical stores and waiting to try on your favorite piece of clothing. The metaverse, powered by cryptocurrency, provides a new dimension to online shopping.

Right from buying costumes for your avatars to investing in real estate, metaverse has a well-defined system for all the transactions.

You can wander around the virtual streets with your friend and enter digital shops to buy anything. You can "try on" clothes, shoes, accessories and a lot more on your personal avatar with the help of 360-degree viewing and virtual augmentation.

The metaverse is not binary. It plans to merge the digital and physical world by offering seamless transaction portals with the help of decentralized commerce.

Let's look at some of the basic things you'll need to take care of to shop in the metaverse.

Create Your Wallet

We talked about how a crypto wallet is literally the virtual embodiment of your leather wallet. You'll be asked to open a crypto wallet and even open an account on significant metaverse platforms, including *The Sandbox* and *Decentraland*.

The wallet will enable the conversion of US Dollars or any other fiat currency into cryptocurrency using your debit or credit cards. Fiat money is a government-issued currency that is not backed by a commodity such as gold. Several crypto exchanges facilitate this conversion in exchange for a nominal fee. Some of the famous ones include Binance and Transak.

Convert Your Fiat Currency Into Crypto

Once you've created the wallet, it is time to put cryptocurrency in it by exchanging with a fiat currency of your choice. Platforms like Binance and Gemini will help you convert these currencies into metaverse coins. On the other hand, crypto like Bitcoin and Ethereum can directly be exchanged for metaverse tokens.

You should keep in mind the volatile trends and market cap of different tokens before investing in them.

Crypto Coins You Can Consider Buying

This entirely depends on the platform you wish to dwell on. Each forum has its own cryptocurrency. However, here are some of the most famous metaverse coins that you can consider buying that work across different virtual setups

Ether - It is the most used currency for digital platform exchanges. Ether is the currency that is responsible for powering the blockchain platform Ethereum. Due to its soaring popularity, Ether can be bought using almost any exchange in the world. In fact, even digital wallet companies like Venmo and Paypal have started allowing users to buy Ether on their platform.

Ether can be used to make purchases across different metaverse platforms since it is not a native coin of any entity.

MANA - It is the native currency of *Decentraland*, a game where you can interact with other players and own land. You can use MANA to buy avatars, lands, and costumes for your character in the game. Since MANA is a DEFI (Decentralized Finance) organization, owning MATA coins will also provide you the right to vote on different aspects of the game, including NFT auctions and policy updates.

Binance, Gate.io, and Kraken are some platforms where you can buy this coin.

AXS - It is the native cryptocurrency of the gaming platform *Axie Infinity*. You can either buy AXS in the usual way through crypto exchanges, or you earn these tokens by breeding digital pets like Axies. These are unique crypto assets that can be used to participate in virtual tournaments and matches.

You can buy AXS on all significant exchange platforms.

SAND - The exclusive token used on the metaverse platform *The Sandbox*, SAND is quite similar in functionality to MANA. You can use it to buy or sell land and other crypto assets in the game's marketplace.

How to Earn Money in The Metaverse

We talked about how the basic money exchange system works in the metaverse. We also talked about how you can spend your money on shopping for different products in the metaverse. Now, it's time to find out how you can actually *make* money in the virtual world economy.

Sounds interesting? Let's get into it.

Here are some of the ways in which you can earn money in the 'verse.

Create Crypto Assets

As a metaverse player, you are not just entitled to buy unique crypto assets, but you can also make your own art pieces and sell them in open marketplaces. The metaverse boasts of several avatars, accessories, collectables, and equipment that are entirely designed by users. This is basically done to encourage the trend of an open economy in the world.

The scope of earning through these assets is not restricted to making your own art piece. You can even open an art gallery and sell other users' work in exchange for a cut in their profit.

Invest in Real Estate

There are literally plots in metaverse platforms like *The Sandbox*, *Decentraland,* and *Axie Infinity* that are sold for millions of dollars. Yes, you heard that right, *millions*!

With such high numbers at play, here are some of the ways you can earn money in the 'verse by investing in virtual real estate.

Real-estate Trading: This refers to the act of buying a virtual piece of land at a low price and selling it at a higher price. Thus, earning the profit made.

Real-estate Brokering: Since virtual property is gathering more popularity day by day, the need for real estate advice is constantly increasing. You can earn commission by making buyers meet sellers or by simply providing advice as a broker.

Managing a Property: Monetize your expertise in the metaverse real estate by becoming a manager of an already existing virtual land. This includes overseeing how virtual venues are being used for concerts and other social events.

Renting Your Property: You can buy land, build a property on it, and rent it to other users, just like you do in real life. Moreover, you can also use your property for providing advertising space to different players.

Real Estate Designing - Just like you can design your own crypto assets, you can create plots of land and bring them to life in the metaverse. The need for 3D designers is well on its way to becoming a necessity for virtual stadiums, shopping malls and private malls.

Advertising - Companies all around the world are rushing to the metaverse to not only boost their virtual presence but also to use it as an advertising platform. You can open your own store in the metaverse and advertise your products across different platforms. As more and more players join the 'verse, the advertising possibilities are only expected to increase.

Gaming

As of 2022, gaming is the most significant part of the metaverse. With the help of blockchain technology and investing in metaverse activities, players can collect in-game assets that one can trade in exchange for tokens that possess real monetary value. Users of the metaverse can also make money by developing games for other players to enjoy.

Big Brands Bringing Big Money into the 'Verse

As a final point, I'd just like to elucidate that if the metaverse is a whirlpool of opportunities, then all major companies would want to get their hands in it. Despite the decentralized nature of transactions, the virtual world has enough scope for companies to generate revenue, probably even more than the real world.

As a result, prominent brands are getting into the mix. This includes Dolce and Gabbana, Adidas, Coca Cola, and Nike. They are even reaching up to an extent where if you buy a real-world product from the company, you stand of chance of gaining the linked crypto asset in the metaverse and vice versa.

Here's an example for the same point. If you buy a designated name-brand to wear to a dance club in the real world, you might also stand a chance to own that particular outfit in the virtual world and wear it to a virtual *The Weeknd's* concert. How cool is that?

As we move forward, there are several ways in which the metaverse business plan might fall in coherence with the physical world. These methods are expected to get complex in the future as more and more people accept and become part of the metaverse. If you see the marketing plans of the real world and metaverse merging in the near future, then you shouldn't be surprised.

It is true that the metaverse hasn't developed yet. But advanced technology foundations like blockchain and crypto assets are setting the stage for a seemingly unbelievable world to come to life.

Conclusion

If you're still unsure as to whether people will be willing to spend their hard-earned money on items that essential aren't really there, think again. The truth of the matter is that they are already willing and more than ready to do exactly that. In 2021, the Earth's population collectively set a record for virtual purchases to the tune of $135 billion. That's a staggering about of money for in-app purchases and equally that $135 billion represents revenues to those entrepreneurs who have laid claim to these new technologies.

Since the metaverse will work much in the same way, it's important to get a head-start on this type of spending. As a member of the metaverse, your money will go towards bettering your avatar and the life you lead in the virtual world. You'll pay to see movies and visit sporting events; you'll also likely spend a good chunk of change prettying up your avatar.

But rather than swiping your credit card, you'll pay via cryptocurrency. As such, you will need to familiarize yourself with buying Bitcoin or other types of crypto, as you can't use cash in the metaverse. The future is digital, and the metaverse is embracing this fact in every facet of its functionality. The good news is that you'll be able to earn crypto in the metaverse, too.

Chapter 4

PROFITING FROM THE METAVERSE

Nobody currently knows for certain what the future of the metaverse looks like. This chapter will be based on recent events, coupled with my perspective, to take a look at a future with the metaverse. A primary conception is that the metaverse will change the world of gaming, but is it limited only to the gaming world? Well, no. There is no doubt that the metaverse will make the gaming business explode; however, there's so much more to it than video games alone. However, gaming is how personal computing and the internet both got started, and they are now fundamentally integrated into society. And so in time the metaverse will become a standard for people to interact with each other and experience different activities, for example watching a football match from the comfort of their home in real-time.

The metaverse will look different depending on who is using it. For example, entrepreneurs, companies, and investors will each use the metaverse differently. Let's take a comprehensive investigation into what the metaverse will look like for these different end-users. Without any further ado, let's dive right in.

Creative Ways for Entrepreneurs to Make Money in the Metaverse

Will the metaverse have completely unfamiliar business models than we have ever seen before? Probably not. With that being said, several unique opportunities will evolve inside this new virtual world. The metaverse is undoubtedly the most mind-blowing invention to come from the 21st century. With the advent of the internet, people have already been exposed to the experience of digital communication, but the metaverse is going to take all of that a notch higher. What does it mean for entrepreneurs? Let's have a look!

You Can Rent Property Virtually

Yes, you heard it right! Can you imagine the concept of virtual renting? It's definitely crazy, but these days, crazy seems to be the norm. Virtual land parcels in the metaverse are somewhat like a blank slate. The owners of these spaces can do whatever they want with their property, including renting it out. Owners enjoy 100% freedom to exercise their creative minds and build their space into a sports stadium, hotel, art gallery, or even a casino!

Once they have built something in their space, the owner would then have the liberty to rent the space out at a premium rate of their choosing. Do you know what this means? You probably have guessed it right—endless revenue opportunities. You can even profit from renting advertising spaces in the virtual world. This brings us to the next point.

You Can Advertise in the Metaverse

Let's assume you have a business in the real world, but you want to reach out to more people. Well, with the metaverse, people will have an abundance of opportunities to interact with brands, companies, and products. This means that entrepreneurs now have a whole new platform to spread awareness about their business. Nowadays, people spend most of their time online. With the advent of the metaverse, this time is only going to increase, giving entrepreneurs the upper hand to ensure enhanced interaction with their target audience.

You Can Invest in Existing Tech Protocols

Most of the metaverses are still being developed on the Ethereum network. The price of ETH is currently skyrocketing, owing to the massive popularity of the metaverse. Entrepreneurs can choose to invest in the existing tech protocols of the metaverse, but keep in mind that it's a volatile world out there.

For example, Solana witnessed huge growth in the past few months made possible because several institutional investors participated and the NFTs soared in popularity. Several factors play into whether investing in tech protocols will offer good returns including NFT demand, blockchain protocols for solving scalability problems, and the cost of network fees.

You Can Make NFT-Based Profits

You may be aware of NFTs, or non-fungible tokens, and how they have taken the world by storm. NFTs possess certain unique technological features and are considered special data pieces that are scarce. We all know that scarcity equals value, right? The same rule applies to NFTs!

It is expected that the value of NFTs will increase over time so you, as an entrepreneur, will stand to make a profit in the long run if you choose to invest in them early. But keep in mind, there is a lot of uncertainty in these assets, similar to how the stock market operates. NFTs hold a good amount of potential, especially now while they are trending; but you should always be careful and do your research before investing.

Need more examples to help you visualize how entrepreneurs will prosper in the metaverse? Here are some simple ideas on how to make your brand thrive in this virtual space –

- Sell virtual products – Here's a piece of exciting information. Did you know that in 2021 alone, over $100 billion was spent on purchasing virtual goods across different gaming platforms? It's true, and this is real money that we are talking about! The main advantage of virtual goods is that you can eliminate the transportation and manufacturing costs that have to be factored into producing physical goods. The most common examples of virtual goods are different in-game items such as skins, tools, or potions.

- Provide VIP access through NFTs – One of the hottest innovations in the tech world is NFTs, and as an entrepreneur, you can use NFTs to offer VIP access. Not sure how? Let's say you are launching a new product or conducting an exclusive event. In that case, you can sell special NFTs before that event and offer VIP access to your customers. For example, Gary Vaynerchuck sold NFTs that provided people a three-year special access pass to VeeCon.

- Build a community – The metaverse will thrive on social commerce – and every entrepreneur should see it as a golden opportunity. Community building is an integral part of marketing your brand, and you can build engaging communities through the metaverse. The metaverse takes virtual engagement to a whole new level.

- Build virtual showrooms – Showrooms offer customers the opportunity to check out products in-depth before they decide to purchase them. Virtual showrooms will make things better since customers can interact with the products from the comfort of their own location. In short, these showrooms can bridge the gap between in-person and online shopping while saving the customer's precious time since commute time is eliminated.

- Reach a new audience – The geographical boundaries of a physical store will no longer be an obstacle with a metaverse store. Virtually anyone can visit your store, regardless of location. It also provides the opportunity for the younger audience to join without requiring a trip to the physical store.

As the metaverse evolves, opportunities for entrepreneurs will also grow. Consider implementing the strategies mentioned above into your marketing plan to ensure that your brand is kept up to par with your competition.

How Can Companies Benefit from the Metaverse?

Now, let's have a look at what virtual reality and the metaverse mean for companies. Many things have happened since Mark Zuckerberg announced the renaming of his highly profitable company, Facebook. He committed to investing millions of dollars into building the turf at Meta.

With this move, Zuckerberg gained the attention of several of his competitors. Microsoft dropped nearly $70 billion as it attempted an acquisition in the gaming industry. Eric Sheridan, of Goldman Sachs, recently mentioned that the metaverse is an "$8 trillion market opportunity." Indeed, that's the equivalent to the GDPs of Japan and Germany combined!

LinkedIn senior editor, Jessi Hempel, made several forecasts about the metaverse. Most of her forecasts are thought-provoking; let's explore some of them. Hempel wrote about the metaverse in the list of 29 big ideas that will change the world. Her forecast described a "metaverse land grab" that has already begun. Let us break all this down.

> *The idea of the metaverse and the use of augmented and virtual reality has been around for decades.*

Several big companies have begun to roll out their own metaverse platforms in a rush so that they don't get left behind in this race. These platforms will include different virtual reality experiences and take users to a different world altogether. On the other hand, these metaverse competitors will also include some augmented reality experiences (an excellent example is Pokémon Go). Get ready for complex video games!

- Hempel speculates that big tech companies will attempt to carve out as much control as they can over the metaverse landscape. A very prominent example is Facebook's rebranding to Meta. Even Microsoft has teased its way into this world with the launch of a Teams product that would allow users to choose avatars to interact with each other virtually.

- According to Hempel, it's not just the tech giants who will benefit from the metaverse. Small companies will also have a significant role; A lot of people agree with her on this. Thanks to blockchain, the metaverse cannot be easily walled-off. A quote from Hempel fits this situation perfectly. She said that the blockchain, "will allow metaverse participants to build and use decentralized technology rather than rely on big tech players alone." In layman's terms, this would mean that creatives and start-ups will get ample opportunities of their own.

So, if you are a small company hoping to make it big on the metaverse, how will you do it? Worry not. Here are some steps that you should consider taking as a small business owner:

- Understand your niche – Before you take any step to adjust to the metaverse, your first task is to know your niche thoroughly. No matter how the world perceives the metaverse, remember that the base concept is nothing new. Zuckerberg might have you believe that this is the next big thing. What he isn't saying is that the idea of the metaverse and the use of augmented and virtual reality has been around for decades. The only difference is that now it is being presented in a well-packaged format ready to be sold to the common people. So, if you want your small business to thrive in this era of virtual transformation, you first need to have a clear idea about what your brand stands for and how you can leverage it. The metaverse will mean different things for different companies, and it is only you who can figure that out.

- Rebranding might be the next step – There are plenty of branding opportunities standing right in front of you. Understanding your niche will help you figure out which path to take. The immense focus on connecting people in the metaverse is something you must keep in mind. Whether you simply want to change your logo or adjust your visuals a little bit, make sure they align properly with you're the brand message that you want to reflect into the metaverse.

- Leverage the initiatives of bigger companies – Did you know that Amazon Web Services has decided to launch a special pilot program to help small businesses enter the world of e-commerce and connect them with new customers? Similarly, some other big names have been making initiatives too. For example, Facebook didn't only change its name to Meta, but it also created some new features for business accounts seeking ways to connect better with audiences. Make sure you are up to date about initiatives that have the potential to elevate your business.

Now that you are more aware of what the metaverse means for companies—big or small—keep in mind that one of the most crucial steps is to maintain your online presence. Without that, you are going to miss out on opportunities that walk right past.

Demystifying the Metaverse for Investors

According to a venture capital CEO, the metaverse stands to become a $10-30 trillion industry in just a decade! You can bet that everyone is looking for a piece of this cake. Investors are no different. If you want to know what investment opportunities are coming up, well, you have come to the right place.

Let's review the three simple ways you can invest and make money from the metaverse. We'll discuss each of these in detail.

Diversify with ETFs

Are you looking for some metaverse exposure? You can start by placing your money in exchange-traded funds, or ETFs, that are specifically targeted on the metaverse. One of the best examples of this is the Roundhill Ball Metaverse ETF. It was brought to market by Matthew Ball.

But how does ETF operate? Operating a full-fledged virtual world requires a LOT of moving parts! To support it all, you need good computational power, proper bandwidth to provide the data, appropriate hardware for worldwide access, payment systems capable of virtual transactions, and means to ensure identity security. All of that is only a snippet of what the actual metaverse ecosystem requires. Thus, there would be several companies involved in supporting this virtual world.

Consider the Roundhill Ball Metaverse ETF, which has a total of 45 holdings at the beginning of February 2022. Can you guess what the median market cap of those holdings is? $68 billion! In simpler words, any random company represented by this ETF stands to be profitable in the long run. These companies not only have prominent ties with the metaverse, but also are very likely to fund the research and development of this virtual world. In short, if you invest your money here, you can sleep well at night knowing that your money is probably going to return you a profit.

The only catch here is that the expense ratio is 0.75%, a little bit higher than average ETFs. However, if the Metaverse indeed lives up to its hype, then the 0.75% net expense ratio would be worth it.

Buy Stocks That Have Metaverse Ties

If you feel that ETFs are not your thing, there are other ways to make bank with the metaverse. You can pick companies that are related to the metaverse and buy their stocks directly.

Now, you may ask, what is the benefit of following this strategy? With this method, you will be investing your money directly into companies, giving you more control. Moreover, most online brokerages have little to no deposit requirements and commission fees are almost non-existent. Compared to ETFs, investing directly with metaverse-friendly companies may have you coming out on top!

On the downside, this strategy may require you to spend hours researching. Or maybe not; most of the companies tied to the metaverse are already well-established, so they are easy to find.

Let me give you an example. Everyone has heard of Microsoft. This corporation has some indirect ways it will benefit when it comes to cloud spending within the metaverse. Azure Microsoft's advanced cloud technology is already in second position. In order to handle huge amounts of data within the metaverse, cloud computing will play a significant role.

https://sensoriumxr.com/articles/best-ways-of-making-money-in-the-metaverseIf you have a high-risk tolerance cap, then maybe this strategy is something you can try out. Look for relevant cryptocurrencies to purchase.

Although most of the companies associated with the metaverse have been established, it's not the same when it comes to cryptocurrencies. Crypto is relatively new and there's no guarantee of long-term performance.

At the same time, *Decentraland* and *The Sandbox* have market values of $4.9 billion and $3.4 billion, respectively. Both of them can be an absolute steal if they keep growing at the same pace because they will capture a significant portion of the market. Following a YOLO strategy, which stands for "you only live once," can work for some investors. The strategy is to invest all your eggs in one basket; the one that you believe will perform the best and have substantial returns. Using this strategy on cryptocurrencies sort of depends on the metaverse being decentralized. Keep in mind that with more prominent companies, like Microsoft, investing billions in the metaverse, there's a chance that the metaverse will turn in the direction of becoming centralized.

Conclusion

Although the hype around the metaverse is growing at a rapid pace, experts believe that there are still many more years to come before it can run at a full pace. People are building the metaverse in bits and pieces and it is still uncertain how everyone will use it. But one thing is for sure, the concept of this new virtual world has opened up different streams of revenue for entrepreneurs, businesses, and investors alike. The sky's the limit when it comes to opportunities in the metaverse.

We must not forget that with metaverse slowly taking form, the competition for innovation is higher than ever before. Meta announced at the beginning of this year that they are building a supercomputer that could be the first foundational stone towards converting the concept of metaverse into reality.

Big businesses have plenty to gain from the metaverse, as discussed in this chapter, but it also brings into question how the safety of its users be safeguarded. Many suspect that Meta will affect young users negatively; but with so many positives, moderation may be the key to safe access for all. With the speed that innovations are coming out today, it may be only a matter of time before avatars and augmented reality become a part of our daily lives in the form of the metaverse.

Chapter 5

CRYPTO IN THE METAVERSE

While it may have felt like something out of a sci-fi action film a decade ago, the metaverse has evolved into a significant element of modern life. In particular, meta-mania gripped the corporate world in 2021, with Facebook launching metaverse-focused projects and creating a plethora of metaverse-related content.

You're undoubtedly familiar with blockchain, cryptocurrencies, and NFTs too, which are now hot subjects. One thing is sure: there is never enough crypto in the metaverse! You'll be inundated with deals, discounts, sales, gadgets, and gizmos, among other things. And you'll want to get your hands on them all!

Following Facebook's announcement of its rebranding to Meta, cryptocurrencies such as MANA, used for trading in the metaverse, saw a 400% price spike.1 What does this imply in the long run? What role does blockchain play in Facebook's metaverse strategy, as well as the global metaverse in general?

To begin addressing these concerns, let us consider what blockchain means in the context of a virtual world like the metaverse.

You might take the metaverse to be a collection of interconnected virtual worlds, similar to the internet but accessible through VR. This is essentially true, but the metaverse also has a key, albeit a little mysterious, aspect that will distinguish it from today's internet: the blockchain.

As already discussed in the previous chapter, Web 3.0 will be the metaverse's foundation. It will be made up of blockchain-enabled decentralized applications that will support a user-owned cryptocurrency and data economy.

Now, blockchain is basically a technology that creates a permanent record of transactions, usually in a decentralized and public ledger. Cryptocurrency is a digital currency or asset that can only be traded online and authenticated by a decentralized blockchain network.

You can use cryptocurrency or "crypto" to make purchases just like traditional currency, but the value of crypto can fluctuate drastically due to its decentralized structure, which means no single entity or set of entities controls or regulates its value. Various cryptocurrencies are available for purchase, including Bitcoin, Ethereum, MANA, and Facebook's foray into the technology. The most well-known blockchain-based cryptocurrency is Bitcoin.

When you buy Bitcoin, for instance, the transaction is recorded on the Bitcoin blockchain, which means the information is spread to thousands of computers all over the world. It is exceedingly tough to deceive or manipulate this dispersed recording system. Moreover, in contrast to traditional banking records, public blockchains such as Bitcoin and Ethereum are transparent—all transactions are visible to anybody on the internet.

The Connection Between Blockchain and the Metaverse

Now, how is the metaverse related with blockchain crypto assets? To begin with, you can use the blockchain to own digital assets in a virtual environment. You'll not only possess that NFT in the real world but also in the virtual one.

Moreover, the metaverse isn't being developed by a single organization or corporation. Separate organizations will create different virtual worlds, eventually interconnecting to form the metaverse. Individuals will want to bring their belongings when they move between virtual worlds, such as Microsoft's and *Decentraland's.*

The blockchain will substantiate proof of ownership of your digital items in both virtual worlds if they are interconnected. Fundamentally, you will have access to your crypto assets till the time you can access your crypto wallet within a virtual environment.

It's easy to see how cryptocurrency could fit into the metaverse's vision. Crypto is utterly distinct from real-world fiat currencies in terms of value and physical form. As a result, it's a convenient way to pay and transact in the virtual world.

Furthermore, by definition, the metaverse is a decentralized system. A single entity must not control the metaverse, and decentralizing its currency would go a long way toward achieving this goal.

Additionally, cryptocurrency and blockchain technology, in general, could serve as a beneficial anchor in an ever-changing virtual environment. Our environs, natural habitats, people's appearances, commodities, and so on would alter in the metaverse based on developer activity and continuing customization. The immutability of blockchain and cryptocurrency would provide much-needed stability.

Use Cases of Blockchain in the Metaverse

Incentives for creators will most likely be one of the first blockchain applications in the metaverse. Epic Games sued Apple in August 2020 for charging a 30% fee for any purchase made through their popular game, *Fortnite*.

In the metaverse, similar problems can arise. The use of cryptocurrency to incentivize creators would ensure that no inconsistent or unfair regulations are directing the exchange. Non-fungible tokens, or NFTs, would effectively become in-game assets that you could earn and sell. Users might then make actual money that has worth in the metaverse by playing VR games. Even if the user exited the game, the game was removed, or there was an unpleasant occurrence in the metaverse, the assets would be wholly unaffected.

Real estate, like in-game assets, is a precious resource in the metaverse. Given the unlimited space and simultaneous users of the metaverse, defining and monitoring real estate can be difficult.

Blockchain can serve as an immutable record of how real estate is generated, edited, transferred, and destroyed in the metaverse.

The metaverse is, in reality, a technological breakthrough, and technology has always been a way to signal affluence. The two worlds have always been relatively interwoven, from the latest cellphones to the most expensive accessories. Even as we've seen more blockchain-based improvements in the previous decade, luxury has been indicated somehow. Cryptocurrencies, which were once a revolutionary internet concept, are now frequently worth thousands of dollars, and possessing them has become a means to display riches, with 'crypto bros' dominating social media. Owning a piece from a top-rated collection is now like owning a Basquiat or a Warhol, thanks to NFTs being used as internet collectibles.

For instance, to commemorate the 200th birthday of Louis Vuitton's founder, the premium label released the game *Louis the Game*. Players can play as Louis Vuitton and search for some of the thirty NFTs hidden throughout the game. Ten of these NFTs were created in partnership with *Beeple*, a well-known digital artist, but none of the thirty will be available for purchase.

The use of blockchain technology also makes it easier to keep track of royalty payments. It not only allows designers to create an irreversible proof of invention, but it can also be used to create and track trademarks, license designs, royalty programs, and sales generated by these designs.

It has been nearly two years since *Fortnite* hosted an exclusive *Star Wars: The Rise of Skywalker* event, during which fans got a sneak peek at the film, got to play with lightsabers, and danced with the director J.J. Abrams' avatar, all while playing the massively popular online game.

Of course, *Fortnite* isn't the only one with a digital venue up and running. The metaverse's added value for entertainment companies comes down to three primary functions: immersive narratives, world-building, and unleashing fan creativity.
These three aspects add to the franchise-building process while increasing audience engagement, two of the most critical factors for any modern entertainment company. Disintermediation, automated micropayments, usage-based payments, and royalty payments are all possible with blockchain in entertainment, all while allowing for a more customer-centric approach by putting control back in the hands of control creators.

Blockchain's immersive applications, on the other hand, aren't simply for consumer-facing industries like entertainment. Blockchain is incredibly beneficial to businesses, too, since it provides them with flexibility, confidentiality, and security. It can be precious for companies seeking efficiency and improved methods to serve customers, as it can be used to perform transactions and raise funds.

In addition, almost every component of the metaverse can be applied to higher education and online learning. Some universities incorporate parts and pieces of metaverse's essential digital tools, including virtual reality, gamification, and leveraging various communication platforms to engage with students and other faculty members. They can also employ blockchain-based cloud services to store critical academic records, curricula, and other data.

Governments are entering the metaverse and delivering public services online as part of the transformation. Metaverse Seoul is developing its public service digital platform, including a virtual city hall, AI-powered public gathering areas, and blockchain-based community services as the first major city to join the metaverse.

Lastly, as individuals move around the metaverse and their identities change, blockchain technology can keep track of them, effectively operating as a virtual version of a social security number. For transparency and to combat crimes in the metaverse, age, changes in appearance, history of online activity, and other unique characteristics can be recorded on the blockchain.

NFTs in the Metaverse

NFTs are hot items. Twitter CEO Jack Dorsey sold his first tweet for $2.9 million, a *Beeple* work of art sold for more than $69 million at a Christie's auction, and Zo Roth, dubbed "Disaster Girl," paid off her undergraduate debt with a $500,000 photo.2

NFT is an abbreviation for 'Non-Fungible Token.' Data is essentially accounted for in a digital ledger and represents a specific item. For instance, it can represent a work of art, a music album, or other forms of digital assets. That's all there is to it, right? Not at all!

When you purchase an NFT, you effectively buy a digital record of a token's ownership that can later be transferred to a digital wallet. A blockchain is a digital record that certifies that token as proof of ownership. This is the same technology used to trade

Bitcoin, Ethereum, Litecoin, and other cryptocurrencies and register their ownership.

However, with an NFT, the token mentioned above has a different meaning.

Let's look at this through the lens of a piece of art. The customer effectively purchases a token that grants them the authority to own the original work. But the actual copyright stays with the original creator or owner.

"Why would anyone buy it?" some would wonder. The motivation appears to be to either own the original work or flip it and resell it for a greater price once it receives some recognition.

Most NFTs are connected to the Ethereum blockchain on a large scale. Ethereum, like bitcoin, is a cryptocurrency, but its blockchain also enables NFTs, which store additional information that allows them to function differently from an ETH coin. Other blockchains can use NFTs as well.

Is NFT Part of the Metaverse?

Almost every metaverse discussion revolves around the possibility of combining metaverse and NFTs. On the other hand, many people believe that NFTs are just another part of the metaverse. Indeed, NFTs and metaverse are frequently used interchangeably.

The primary rationale for these assumptions is that NFTs in the blockchain gaming industry have experienced unexpected growth bursts. It is logical to assume that only virtual worlds will shape the metaverse. By serving the virtual worlds, interoperable games can help to foster metaverse development.

Furthermore, the link between real-life identities and digital avatars opens up possibilities for using NFTs to define access to the metaverse. With NFT-controlled access in 2019, the metaverse NFT token appeared first.

Thanks to a good yardstick, many new projects have emerged in recent decades to capitalize on the convergence of NFTs and the metaverse. The initiatives are primarily focused on introducing significant changes in online interaction approaches.

What distinguishes NFTs from Crypto?

NFTs are sometimes misunderstood as a type of cryptocurrency. NFTs and crypto are both based on blockchain, and both use the same technology and principles. As a result, they tend to draw the same types of people. NFTs are a subset of the crypto culture, and you'll almost always need cryptocurrency to buy and sell them.

Crypto and NFTs are comparable in that they both have a digital trail maintained on a blockchain. The parallels cease there. The fundamental distinction is evident in the name. Cryptocurrency is a currency. It has only economic value and is fungible (exchangeable), just like any other currency.

This means that no matter which crypto token you hold within a particular cryptocurrency, it has the same value as the next. Due to this, the worth of cryptocurrency is more explicit; for instance, you may trade one bitcoin for another. Every token of equal price can be exchanged for another.

On the other hand, each token in the NFT system is non-fungible, has a distinct value, and cannot be swapped for another of the same value.

Fun and Games

The metaverse is an alternate reality. It may not appear to be one at first, but it will rapidly take on a life of its own as more users join. Once inside, there's an almost limitless number of things to do, not least of which are fun and games. Gaming will likely be one of the most intriguing uses for the metaverse, and blockchain will once again drive innovation in this field.

Prepare to be blown away by metaverse gaming!

The Sandbox is a virtual world where anybody can develop their games and environments and purchase and trade digital commodities and assets using the Ethereum-based blockchain money $Sand. *The Sandbox* is already home to well-known firms, like Atari and Aardman Animations, developers of *Shaun the Sheep*.

Crypto gaming is already a significant business and involves both online casino-style games as well as the more modern gaming model that's become known as "play-to-earn." One of the most prominent is *Axie Infinity*, wherein over a million daily active users train and combat artificial monsters analogous to *Pokémon Go*. It varies from Nintendo's game in that winners are given the cryptocurrency SLP, with the best earning around $250 each day - a substantial sum in the underdeveloped countries where the game is extremely popular!

Oneto11, which bills itself as the world's first blockchain-based gaming environment, is another metaverse game where players can earn cryptocurrency that is convertible to actual money. Players contest for the platform's blockchain token, also known as Oneto11, by using their sports acumen to compete against others.

We can expect blockchain gaming to blow up in the next few years if the metaverse lives up to its hubbub, as everyone from Mark Zuckerberg to tech venture capitalists believe.

Conclusion

For years, cryptocurrencies such as Bitcoin and Ethereum have dominated the headlines. But what is blockchain technology, exactly? What is the mechanism behind it? And what are our options for dealing with it?

Consider games to illustrate how blockchain technology has become a revolutionary method to construct and interact with digital landscapes. Many parts of the metaverse will be affected by blockchain technology since you will need to build your crypto collection to harness the metaverse's potential fully.

With the increased interest in NFTs, you may expect them to become more common in the metaverse. Cryptocurrencies and NFTs could have various applications in the metaverse, including virtual education, business, government, entertainment, and fashion. And, since gaming will undoubtedly be a mainstay of the metaverse, these forms of currency will almost certainly be used in conjunction with it.

In-game and in-app purchases now account for astounding sums of money. As a result, it's only natural to use our crypto to make comparable purchases in the metaverse. You might think that all of this is pointless right now. It can come out as a little ridiculous.

However, once you start using the metaverse regularly, you're likely to change your mind. Whatever the case may be, it's understandable if you find yourself questioning the metaverse's necessity.

Chapter 6

FROM THE SILVER SCREEN TO YOUR VR HEADSET

It's easy to draw comparisons to many sci-fi movies when looking at the metaverse. One doesn't have to look far, either, to see just how closely Zuckerberg's vision rivals many blockbuster movies. Indeed, the metaverse will remind most people of movies like 1999's instant classic, *The Matrix*. For those unfamiliar, the Matrix movie franchise is one of the most popular film series in science fiction history. It was created by the Wachowskis and has in some way or another impacted the lives of millions of people over the years with its intriguing story and captivating action sequences. If you're a fan of the movies, you know what they mean for science fiction as a whole.

The Matrix single-handedly changed the way action movies are made. It introduced groundbreaking effects like "Bullet Time," for example. Bullet Time was a slow-motion, multi-camera film technique that was used to create an amazing sense of speed during fight scenes. The Wachowskis also used digital effects a lot throughout the Matrix movies, which made it possible to create realistic-looking animations and computer graphics. And then there were the action sequences. These scenes effectively breathed new life into the genre in ways that defied traditional movie-making techniques. But as incredible as all these film techniques and computer effects were at the time, it's the story that's stood the test of time the best. To this day, lines from the Matrix movies are regularly used in everyday vernacular, and understandably so.

The Matrix films perfectly encapsulated the idea that we might be living in a computer-generated world. They've since spawned numerous fan theories about the Matrix universe and our own. To say *The Matrix* had a significant impact on society would be a gross understatement and a disservice to the Wachowskis. The sheer complexity and intrigue of the stories they came up with were enough to carry a franchise for over two decades (*The Matrix Resurrections* just released in December 2021). Not to mention the rabid fan base and new perspective the movies gave us on life as we know it.

In *The Matrix*, the main character learns he is living in a simulation. It soon becomes clear that those in the Matrix can instantly download knowledge and information to their avatars, making it possible to learn advanced martial arts or how to fly a helicopter in a matter of seconds. The lines between realities begin to blur just a bit when discussing life in the Matrix, and the same is true for the metaverse. In both worlds, the user gets transported to a lifelike reality that offers all new possibilities. In the metaverse, much of the real world is present if you want it to be. But there are additional layers that help enhance our own reality. Conversely, you can use the metaverse to take you to places not possible in the real world, thus using the wonders of VR and AR to immerse you in a new dimension.

An interesting plot point regarding the Matrix has to do with the fact that some people were fully aware of the false world that the Matrix provided and were completely fine with it. They chose to let themselves get lost in the false reality and live out the rest of their lives in blissful ignorance. Could this be a sign of things to come for the metaverse? All you have to do is look at the hold that smartphones have on a vast majority of the population to see how addicting technology can be if one allows it. Given that the metaverse is exponentially more engrossing than your average smartphone or video game, there will undoubtedly be those who choose to live out their lives in it as much as possible. Is this a dangerous proposal? Or will there be safeguards in place that help its users balance their realities? Time will tell.

So while *The Matrix* gave us a glimpse into the possibility of living in a VR world, nothing is quite as on-the-nose as 2018's *Ready Player One*. The film started out as a novel by author Ernest Cline but quickly became a blockbuster hit with the help of Steven Spielberg. The movie adaptation helps connect the dots as to what the computer-generated world of the metaverse could look like once complete. Interestingly, *Ready Player One* takes place in the not-too-distant future of 2045. In its universe, Earth is a dystopia that's on the brink of total ruin. As such, there aren't too many pleasant destinations in the real world. So, the vast majority of the planet's inhabitants seek respite in the "OASIS," a computer-generated world that sounds eerily similar to the metaverse. 1

People strap on VR headsets and other gear in order to log into the OASIS. Once there, they meet up with friends and other OASIS users. The worlds around them are entirely digital, allowing players to do everything from the mundane to the insane. In one scenario, a bunch of different players are getting together in an attempt to win a race. The winner of this race receives an "Easter egg" for their troubles. As per the plotline, winning enough challenges ultimately wins ownership of the OASIS, as its original creator died. Prior to his death, however, the creator implemented a contest to play out postmortem where he challenges the OASIS's users to compete in various trials he created to win control of the

OASIS. While you shouldn't expect Zuckerberg to do the same in the metaverse, you can see clear parallels between these two digital worlds when you look beyond *Ready Player One*'s plotline and focus on the inner workings of the novel/film's universe.

It's rather compelling seeing just how much was considered when bringing the OASIS to life. Players are inundated with ads, promotions, and new things to buy for their digital counterparts, known as avatars. In the OASIS, players can buy everything from clothes to vehicles and just about everything in-between. Some digital purchases are purely cosmetic, allowing the player to present themselves in an entirely new, albeit fictional, light. Others, however, give the player an edge in the digital games they play in the OASIS, much like today's video games.

Over in the metaverse, things are shaping up to mirror the OASIS in more ways than one. If you've seen the *Ready Player One* movie, it's safe to say that you have a pretty solid concept of how the metaverse will operate. But whereas the OASIS is more of an escape from reality, the metaverse is meant to complement it.

An Entirely New Matrix

Much how *The Matrix* was set in a dystopian reality, *Ready Player One* is set in a universe where the real world is not a very inviting place. And while the metaverse clearly borrows from many of these movies' core concepts, it's not meant to be a replacement for the world we live in. Rather, the metaverse aims to offer a completely new matrix for people to inhabit, and one that its users will frequently travel back and forth between—at least, for the time being.

Remember, VR has been around for decades. But it wasn't until recently that the technology was affordable enough to reach the masses. Now, virtual reality headsets are so popular that they're quickly becoming a hot commodity among generations past and present. Still, it's going to take some time before most of the population owns a VR system. Mr. Zuckerberg would undoubtedly like that to happen sooner rather than later. But realistically, it's likely to be a slow process until enough people sign up for the metaverse and sing its praises. Once word gets out, it's a pretty safe bet that VR sales will ramp up exponentially.

Now, you previously read where worlds like the Matrix and the OASIS served as escapes for its players. While it's true that the metaverse isn't *intended* to be a replacement to everyday life, it's kind of hard to imagine it not playing out as such. Think about it; there's a lot of strife going on worldwide right now. The media is flush with negative reports on a near-daily basis. You certainly wouldn't be criticized for wanting to seek refuge in a far-off world. And that's the beauty of the metaverse. You can access those kinds of places without ever leaving your home.

And with the world becoming more digital every day, the metaverse and its VR gateway make it possible to break free from all of the negativity in the world. Now, it's easy for detractors of these technologies to allude to their counterintuitive side effects on the human psyche. After all, the metaverse could easily become an addiction, just like video games, smartphones, and the many other forms of media. But VR is being used for good, as well. It's playing important roles in medical fields, military training, and even as a form of therapy for people with mental illnesses. VR is also now being used by brands to show their products in an immersive way that would otherwise be impossible without it.

When you look at the metaverse next to *Ready Player One* or *the Matrix*, it's only natural to draw comparisons and assume that Zuckerberg's creation will mimic what we see on the silver screen. But one must look deeper into the metaverse to see its benefits to our reality. What was once only dreamed possible by some of our most creative thinkers is now on the cusp of worldwide release. The metaverse is truly a momentous breakthrough that deserves to be viewed through its own lenses and not those portrayed in movies. It's fun to point out similarities, but the metaverse will change our outlook on life in more ways than one.

If you want to see where VR has been and where it's going, look no further than the medical industry. VR has been used in medical fields for years. Doctors have used it to train surgeons, nurses, and other types of healthcare professionals. For example, many medical universities are training with VR technology to help budding physicians learn how to perform complicated surgeries. Moreover, virtual reality helps surgeons prepare for different scenarios that might occur during surgery. This not only gives them more confidence but also makes it easier for them to learn how to deal with potential complications.2 Now imagine how much farther we can take those advancements with a living, breathing platform like the metaverse. Until the metaverse came along, collaborating on scientific breakthroughs and medical advancements was limited to academic settings. Once the metaverse is in full gear, virtually anyone can share their ideas in real-time and discuss ways to improve the world of medicine, education, sports, and more.

The military is another entity that's long been using virtual reality. They use the technology to assist in training soldiers in warfare and other real-world scenarios. And VR therapy has proven to be an effective form of treatment for people suffering from mental illnesses like PTSD or depression because it's immersive enough that patients feel like they're living through events all over again—helping them heal emotionally while making the process less jarring than traditional therapy sessions.

Keep in mind that virtual reality is a multibillion-dollar industry, and it's one of the most profitable new technologies to emerge over the last few decades. In 2020, VR's revenues were at $1.8 billion globally. In 2022, that number is predicted to increase by as much as 30%. Along with the technology itself, there are many diverse areas of VR-related industries that contribute to its economic impact. These include hardware manufacturing, gaming hardware manufacturing, software development, content creation, and much more. The economic implications of VR are clear. It's not only an innovative technology that is financially prosperous for those in its industry—but it also has many other benefits to society, as well, and ones that Mark Zuckerberg is fully intending to take advantage of in order to see his vision for metaverse come to fruition.

> *How we take the metaverse to task is entirely up to us.*

Yes, movies like *The Matrix* and *Ready Player One* make VR worlds seem everything from scary to fun. But in (virtual) reality, the metaverse is going to be so much more, and the benefits of VR are proving that on an ongoing basis. Thanks to VR and all that it's capable of, the metaverse is positioned to alter the course of mankind going forward—it's that revolutionary. How we take the metaverse to task is entirely up to us. As it stands, Zuckerberg's vision is to give the people of this planet both an alternative and a companion to daily life. If we accept the metaverse with open arms and a willingness to help it grow, we can make it our own matrix— one that's far from a dystopian wasteland and closer to a digital paradise full of possibilities.

But is that possible? It's important to remember that we had the same vision for the internet all those years ago. As we discussed a couple of chapters ago, the internet was at one time new, exciting, and full of possibilities. Fast-forward to today, however, and it's safe to say that many people have grown tired of the internet. Rather than being used for expanding knowledge, the average consumer uses the internet for nothing more than mindless entertainment and arguing over trivial matters. It's hardly revered as the revolutionary technology that we saw it as when it first came out.

But perhaps that's to be expected. Maybe all technologies get boring after a while. And the same might eventually happen with the metaverse. It certainly doesn't have to, but it's highly probable based on the track record of the average consumer. Rarely do we use technology for its intended vision. Instead, we drone on about looking for the next best thing. And when it comes along, we don't use it at its full potential. Could the metaverse be different? It's certainly possible, especially when you stop to consider all that it's said to be capable of. There's a chance that the only concern metaverse users will have is upgrading their VR gear to the latest and greatest, much like many consumers do with smartphones.

And you can bet that VR equipment will have a big share of the market once the metaverse gets rolling. If you've had the pleasure of using different VR systems, you know that some are far more capable than others. The quality of your VR gear will dictate the level of realism and immersiveness of the metaverse. So if you want to experience the metaverse to its fullest potential, you're going to want to invest in VR tech that's on the bleeding edge of innovation. Advanced VR technology isn't cheap. But those who wish to truly immerse themselves in the metaverse likely won't mind the expense.

We see the same thing right now with video games, TVs, phones, and cars. So, what makes VR any different? What's more, there are some people who will pay any price to achieve the separation from reality that the metaverse promises to provide. There are those who prefer a life of isolation and solitude. With the metaverse, you won't ever have to leave your house if you don't want to. The metaverse will bring the needs of the outside world right into your home. It's yet another testament to the personalization offered through the metaverse. If you don't want to talk to anyone, you certainly don't have to. Conversely, you can go full-on Matrix and thrive in a living, breathing world that's full of other avatars with which you can freely interact.

Speaking of *The Matrix*, users of the metaverse will undoubtedly want to experience things that a VR headset on its own can't provide, such as tactile feedback. And there's no doubt that there are companies out there that are all too happy to oblige. There's already technology in the works that lets VR users "feel" what they're picking up in the virtual world. It's safe to assume that this kind of tech will eventually go far beyond simple tactile experiences, which opens up a whole new can of moral worms. Adult industries are certain to take part in the virtual experiences that VR affords. Combined with the sensory-based technology that's trying to make it to market as we speak, we could be on the cusp of an entirely new way to mingle.

Already, there are inventions on the horizon that connect to existing VR headsets to offer users "something more." One such invention is the FeelReal. Intended to provide smells, heat, and air, the FeelReal is undoubtedly only the beginning of what's sure to become a monstrous enterprise. But do we really have anything to worry about?

 Remember when computers started going down in price to where more people could afford one? It was then that the industry saw a deluge of senseless add-ons, many of which were nothing more than gimmicks designed to make a quick buck. The same was certainly true for the Nintendo Entertainment System (NES) back in the 1980s. Countless cheap accessories were built and sold by third-party companies in an effort to "enhance" the player's experience. In the end, though, the vast majority of them wound up to be utterly useless. Anyone remember the U-Force? Look it up. 3

The point is that the real fun has always been with the original hardware. Very rarely do add-ons and third-party accessories do anything groundbreaking for the hardware on which they are running. If you're still not convinced, think back to when you bought your first smartphone. Do you remember how many gimmicky phone cases and accessories you bought for it? How many of those do you still use? An educated guess would be "Not many."

Still, you should prepare yourself for the same thing all over again once VR and the metaverse become the de facto user experience. But then again, this is an entirely new medium that is still largely untapped and not fully understood. Developers and creators are certain to uncover new possibilities the longer we use VR, AR, and the metaverse. It's possible that we'll find new uses for the metaverse that haven't yet been dreamed of. And at that point, there very well could be a need for hardware enhancements to further our online experience. But until then, it's probably a good idea to watch from afar and take a wait-and-see approach to anything new that third-party companies try to shove down your throat.

You'll be told it's the best thing to ever happen to the metaverse and that you absolutely need it to make the most of your user experience. But before you run out and jump on the bandwagon, give those new toys some time to see how they really turn out.

Conclusion

Over the years, there have been countless movies and TV shows that have given us glimpses into the future, whether we realized it at the time or not. Movies like *The Matrix* and *Ready Player One* showed us what life would be like when the peoples of the planet had access to computer-generated worlds. The fantastical creations of these worlds provided an escape for some but proved to be a burden for others. Could the metaverse's users experience the same fate?

In *The Matrix*, there was a paradox where some people enjoyed the false reality and embraced it, while others craved the real world and the possibilities it presented. In *Ready Player One*, the vast majority of the population preferred the escape from reality that its VR/AR world provided them. With the way things are headed in our reality, it's not a stretch to predict the metaverse providing the same escape for many users.

Of course, movies only give us so much information for what's to come. We need to look at another form of media if we wish to truly see the bigger picture: video games. This digital media will play a significant role in the metaverse, so it's only fair to consider the impact that it's had on society over the years.

Chapter 7

THE SIMS IN YOUR LIVING ROOM

Many people who are looking to draw comparisons to the metaverse often go right to the movies. But there's another medium that deserves equally as much attention: video games. Video games have long been understood as a way to escape from reality—a way to forget the stressors of daily life and zone out in a distant world, fighting enemies and saving princesses. It would therefore be a grave disservice to the metaverse not to include video games among its list of inspirations. As we discussed with *Ready Player One*, the OASIS is largely centered on the concept of playing games to pass the time and forget the woes of life. And while the metaverse will be its own thing, you can bet that it's going to incorporate plenty of leisure in the form of video games.

There is perhaps one video game in particular that helps to bridge the gap between reality and gameplay, and that's *The Sims*. *The Sims* franchise has been around for more than 20 years now, with its initial release dating back to 2000. In this long-running video game series, you were responsible for leading the life of digital characters, appropriately called "Sims." These tiny digital people made up the Sims universe. You could spend the day at your Sims' job, earning money to help finance your Sims' house. You could fall in love with another Sim and start a family—the possibilities seemed limitless at the time. Since *The Sims* was released, it has gone on to produce numerous sequels, expansions, and a rabid community of loyal followers.

Fast-forward to 2009 when *The Sims 3* was released. This game introduced new features like open-world gameplay and the ability to use many more items to customize your Sim. Just with these few descriptions of the game, it's easy to see how the world of *The Sims* ties in with the metaverse. As we've already discussed, you'll be able to customize your avatar to include a number of skins, styles, clothes, and more. What was made popular by *The Sims* will be an everyday thing in the metaverse. And you had better believe that it's going to be huge. Many users will spend big bucks to make their digital counterparts look how they want. And it's going to cost real-world money to bring your metaverse avatar to life. Granted, there will likely be base designs that come included with the metaverse, much like *The Sims* games did. But if you want your avatar to be unique among the many other characters roaming the metaverse, you're going to have to spend some money to make it possible. Again, not too different from *The Sims*. 1

So, what makes *The Sims* such a worldwide hit? At their core, *The Sims* games offer a chance to manage a virtual life. It's why the franchise is found in the life simulation genre. There's something relaxing about taking control of a tiny video game character and running their life. Perhaps it's because it allows the player to forget about their own life challenges while subconsciously "fixing" them through the game. If ever there was a game that made that concept possible, it was *The Sims*. It must have worked, too, because *The Sims* franchise has sold more than 200 million copies of its games worldwide. In addition to being one of the bestselling PC games, there have been different console versions released over the years, from PS2 to Xbox 360 to Nintendo DS. The latest release in the franchise, *The Sims 4*, launched in 2014 after a lengthy development process. It was met with mixed reviews upon release, as some felt it did not offer enough new content, while others appreciated the more streamlined gameplay. Again, this is the potential challenge that the metaverse faces and one that all video game series face at some point in their run.

But unlike *The Sims* when it was released back in 2000, the metaverse has the advantage of patches and updates that install automatically. Such luxuries didn't exist when The Sims first came out. Today, if software requires a critical update, such as to fix a bug or improve on gameplay, the developers can release a patch that effectively fixes the issue. Perhaps the most notable use of this benefit was with the release of 2020's *Cyberpunk 2077*. Projected to be one of the biggest games of all time, *Cyberpunk 2077* turned out to be a buggy mess upon release. So much so that the game was largely unplayable. And due to the litany of problems that plagued the game, gamers around the world launched a lawsuit against its developer, CDProjekt RED.

But even messes like *Cyberpunk 2077* can prove profitable. The game had a massive budget of more than $300 million—a budget that eclipsed many Hollywood blockbusters. And CDProjekt RED made back its budget in just one day of sales. That's how big *Cyberpunk 2077* was believed to be. It wasn't until players fired up the game and started playing it that reality started to settle in. The class-action lawsuit ultimately only cost CDProjekt RED $1.85 million. One has to believe that their settlement was so low due to the promise to patch the game to something playable. At least, that's what the company says it plans to do. As of November 2021, *Cyberpunk 2077* remains problematic. There are still issues within the game that need to be fixed. But CDProjekt RED has already made significant improvements to the game, thanks to numerous patches and updates.

Back in 2004, expansion packs were all that *The Sims* series could rely on to add content to its games. Of course, every Sims game that's been released has been complete and fully playable—they never suffered the same unfinished bugs that plagued *Cyberpunk 2077*. But it's those expansion packs that helped keep interest in the Sims franchise fresh. This is extremely important for video games in general. And it's going to be equally important for the metaverse to implement strategies that entice users to invest in its video game side. Because the metaverse has access to technology that didn't exist in the early days of *The Sims*, it is safe to assume that updates won't be an issue. In fact, they will most likely be a regular thing for the metaverse. Users should expect regular updates, much like we see with the *Windows* operating system.

The legacy of *The Sims* cannot be discounted when it comes to inspiration for the metaverse. Just in *The Sims 4* alone, the game is currently one of the most popular in the series' history, and it continues to be to this day. In fact, there are more than 36 million *Sims 4* players worldwide. *The Sims* franchise has been going strong for over 20 years now. And while the games have changed a lot over the years, there's a lot of history to be learned from the games that the metaverse and its users can use to their advantage. This is important to note, as it gives us a glimpse into the ever-expanding world of online video game communities. What's more, it lets us get a feel for how the metaverse will reach people around the world. Throughout its 20+ year history, *The Sims* franchise has grown and evolved. It's likely that the metaverse will attract many more users compared to *The Sims* as a whole. And in doing so, the metaverse will break all kinds of records in the process.

There are many other video games that deserve mention here. The *Grand Theft Auto* (*GTA*) franchise is certainly among them. While geared toward a more mature audience, *GTA* spawned an entirely new take on video games, one that let players act out fantasies never before possible. The free-roaming world of *GTA* further expanded on what video games could be, marking the dawn of a new era of gameplay. In fact, the 3D worlds of *Grand Theft Auto* don't look too different from those found in the metaverse. Whether the adult material of *GTA* eventually makes its way into the metaverse remains to be seen. But it would be surprising if it didn't. Sex sells, and Rockstar Games, the company behind *GTA*, knew that fact well. It might take a while to find a home in the metaverse, but adult content is sure to follow at some point in time.

For now, though, the metaverse is unlikely to stray too far from *The Sims* or a game like *Minecraft*. The younger generation of gamers spent countless hours mining away in the pixelated world of *Minecraft*, and it's easy to see why. This popular video game let players create and explore their own 3D worlds. The game was (and still is) deceptively simple, but there are numerous challenges in the blocky world. Not only that, but *Minecraft* offered a level of surreal escapism that even the most graphically-advanced games hadn't been able to achieve at the time. And that's a big part of what made the franchise so popular. There's a reason *Minecraft* holds the title of the best-selling video game of all time by a wide margin.2 To date, it's sold a staggering 238 million copies worldwide. Interestingly, *Grand Theft Auto V* is in second place, with 155 million copies sold.

Now, you might be thinking that *The Sims* should be between *Minecraft* and *GTA V*, but it's important to remember that those 200 million copies that *The Sims* sold are for the entire franchise. That puts into perspective just how popular *Minecraft* on its own has fared. For a single title to sell 238 million copies will forever etch *Minecraft*'s name in the history books. If you've never played *Minecraft*, it's grossly addicting. But it's the simplicity and ingenious game design that propelled it to stardom.

Even more impressive is the fact that *Minecraft* started out as an indie game. That means it was created by an amateur game developer without the luxury of a team of expert programmers. Created by Markus Persson, *Minecraft* started off as a PC game in 2009. Now, it has been released for many other gaming consoles. Its popularity led to its eventual releases on home consoles like the Xbox 360, Xbox One, PlayStations 3 and 4, Wii U, PlayStation Vita, and Nintendo Switch. You can also play it on your phone with the Minecraft app. With so many ways to play, you're bound to find one that will suit you best.

Minecraft can be played solo or by up to four players online or offline. There are many modes of gameplay, too, including survival mode, where you have to gather resources and build shelter; creative mode, where there are no health limits and you don't have to deal with mobs; and adventure mode, which is similar to survival but adds exploration and questing aspects. *Minecraft* has been around for about ten years. It's popular for the many reasons already discussed, but not the least of which is how it can be used to create and explore 3D worlds. The fact that it's so customizable, and can be played in many different ways, makes it a good choice for players of all ages and skill levels.

One of the best parts about *Minecraft* is that it's a game that encourages creativity. You really can build anything you want, as the only limiting factor is your own imagination.

There are different materials that you can use to build with, each with its own pros and cons. Wooden planks, for example, are one of the most common blocks in the game. They're pretty weak, so they should be used as support for other materials rather than as a building material itself. Stone has a lot more strength than wood, but it also costs twice as much. It's worth it if you're going to need a lot of strong building materials, though, because it's a great choice for stability. Glass lets light through and looks very nice, but it won't hold up like other materials.

And that's only a sampling of what's found in the game. But it's the sheer variety of objects and the ability to customize your own worlds with them that helped make *Minecraft* the raving success that it's known as today. You don't just climb to the top of the best-selling video game list without offering something special and unique. And *Minecraft* does that in spades. It's going to be important for the metaverse to offer the same appeal, and so far, it looks like it's on track to do just that.

But what else makes a universe like the metaverse appealing to gamers and non-gamers alike? You can already find many different types of life simulation games on the internet. And there are some qualities that stand out that make them so popular. As we've already discussed, a game like *The Sims* has great graphics and fluid animations. It also has many different aspects to it, so there is always something new for players to explore.

Another quality of a good life simulation game is how much detail goes into the environment. The more detailed the environment, the more fun players will have exploring the world and seeing what they can do with it. Something else that's important in a good life simulation game is keeping it fresh and updating it over time. One way developers do this is by adding new features or items to keep players interested in playing their games for longer periods of time. Lastly, a good life simulation game should be intuitive and easy to understand without needing to read tutorials on how to play it or getting frustrated with complicated mechanics or controls.

It's very likely that the metaverse will require a learning curve for its users. It may take some users a considerable amount of time to get used to VR and how it operates, not to mention the ins and outs of the metaverse. But once users get accustomed to this new world, it's sure to offer experiences that have so far been unmatched by even the best video games of all time. Over time, we're sure to see updates that further improve on these experiences, ensuring a lasting virtual journey into the uncharted lands of the metaverse.

Room for Everyone

So far, we've looked at the many connections between the metaverse and the games that got us this far. But one aspect of the metaverse that we've not really delved into is just now vast and expansive it will be. Imagine a new world where you can meet anyone, go anywhere, and do anything—a world without any boundaries. You could be on top of Mount Everest with your best friend from college, or maybe take a stroll through the streets of Paris with your favorite actor.

You are no longer constrained by time or geography. You are free to go anywhere all at once. That's the metaverse—a virtual reality that will change the way we live and work forever. With such attractive possibilities, it stands to reason that the vast majority of the earth's population will want to take part in them. But does the metaverse have the room to support and accommodate so many people? Like the internet, there isn't a limit to how many people can use the metaverse. At least, not right now. It's true that some websites don't have the bandwidth to support a significant influx of people. There are many instances where websites have crashed due to a sudden rush of traffic, such as consumers trying to buy concert tickets.3

But for the most part, popular websites have the means to support high volumes of traffic. The metaverse will of course be somewhat different in this regard. For starters, its users won't simply be logging in to check out something and then log off. No, people are going to be "living" in the metaverse, day and night. As such, there need to be complex systems powering the metaverse behind the scenes. Given that Mark Zuckerberg is pumping $10 billion into his new creation, it's safe to assume that the metaverse will have the support it needs to house millions of users at any given time.

> *It's unlike anything we've seen to date, and it's going to revolutionize the way we interact with one another.*

And therein lies the wonder and magic of the metaverse. There really will be room for everyone, allowing users to create and build their own universes within; personal, shareable worlds that everyone can take part in and explore. It's unlike anything we've seen to date, and it's going to revolutionize the way we interact with one another. Such an experience couldn't have come at a better time. The ongoing pandemic, politics, racial divide, and other factors have culminated in a world that is less united than it's ever been. If we ever needed an innovative solution to our division, it's now. The metaverse stands to strip away our prejudices and unite us once more. Indeed, the metaverse deserves praise on this front. It has many detractors who believe it could lead to the fall of society (more on this later), but we can't overlook the fact that, in the metaverse, things like identity, race, religion, and other characteristics won't matter.

As we've discussed, you can be anyone—or anything—you want to be in the metaverse. Your avatar can be anything you can dream of, allowing other avatars to look past our true identities. Such circumstances could certainly hold the key to resolving the current rifts we face throughout society. Like all new technologies and innovations, there will always be those who are against change. Already, the metaverse has been met with equal praise and disgust. But before judgment begins, it's important to consider our current state of affairs across the planet. The pandemic caused and is causing many parts of the world to stay indoors. As a result, many people are unfairly imprisoned in their own homes, unable to take part in some much-needed human experiences. All of a sudden, however, the metaverse is announced as a way to connect with those we love and others without having to risk infection in the real world.

The timing is perfect for this technology. And the fact that the metaverse wasn't possible until now further illuminates its timing. VR technology alone has advanced exponentially. It is no longer just for gaming.

So, with so many users active at any given time, who will use the metaverse? In short, it will be for anyone and everyone. No matter your profession, the metaverse can offer you new ways to do your job better. Architects can walk through their buildings before they are built. Doctors could even perform surgery remotely with expert help from around the world. The possibilities are endless.

At this juncture, we know that the metaverse will change how we live and work. With the ability to meet anyone, go anywhere, and do anything, it's no wonder that virtual reality is at the forefront of the technology revolution. And with the metaverse behind the VR, we can leave behind our office buildings and enjoy work from home. Our houses can become spaces for friends and family to come together. We can travel to any place we want without worrying about time or money.

Virtual reality will also change what we know as entertainment, as well as sports and news coverage—all of which will take on a whole new dimension. It may be hard to imagine now, but there was a time when people believed we would never surpass movies like *Jurassic Park* or video games like *Skyrim*. Times are changing, and they've changed an awful lot in the past few years. It's somewhat intimidating to think about where we will be technologically in five years. What about ten? And how will our technological advances affect life in the metaverse? It's likely that Zuckerberg and Co. have the metaverse mapped out for the foreseeable future, with fail-safes and other contingencies in place to foster its growth and inevitable expansion.

Conclusion

If there's one game that encapsulates life in the metaverse, it's *The Sims*. But instead of controlling various avatars and dictating their daily lives, you will *be* the avatar. *The Sims* was a monumental milestone in gaming history. Today, it stands as a foretelling reminder of what's to come for all who carry out their lives in the metaverse. Whether in real life or in video games, both realities have given a large portion of the population the tools necessary for managing a virtual life.

If *The Sims* showed people how to lead a balanced life, then games like *Minecraft* gave us insights into building a life of our own and surviving off the land. And if those cases are true, then *Grand Theft Auto* provided a glimpse into a lifestyle that allowed users to act out their wildest dreams without consequences.

Moreover, the staggering popularity of these games proves that there is a significant want for alternate realities. The metaverse aims to fulfill these desires and so much more. And the manner in which it achieves them is nothing short of intriguing. With possible applications ranging from leisure to learning, the metaverse will be rife with opportunities to make the most of its 3D world.

Chapter 8

THE APPLICATIONS OF THE METAVERSE, SO FAR

The metaverse is the next frontier in digital spaces. Currently, we use tools like email, instant messaging, or Facebook to communicate with others. But these online components don't let you feel like you're really there with the people you converse with. That's where the metaverse comes in. The virtual, three-dimensional field of the metaverse provides a space for people to share ideas and interests. It's a place that fosters creativity, collaboration, and even social change. The world is on the cusp of this new era where virtual worlds are just as real as ours. And it won't be long before you can go anywhere without ever leaving your home. With so much potential, there's no question that unique and innovative uses of the metaverse remain largely untapped.

With the information we have so far, we know the metaverse is destined to help bridge the gap between work and home. In the ongoing aftermath of the global pandemic, those fortunate enough to have kept their jobs have transitioned from their office building to their kitchen at home. If you are one of the millions who now work from home, you know the disconnect that it presents. On the one hand, it's great to have the ability to spend more time with your loved ones. But on the other hand, you aren't as connected to your employer as you once were. Being away from the office presents a divide that has its pros and cons. But most employees would agree that something is missing now that they are working from home.

Try as your employer might, *Zoom* meetings are a far cry from interoffice collaborations and brainstorming sessions. Without that physical connection, something is lost. For all intents and purposes, the metaverse looks like it's going to remedy this widespread issue by placing users in a virtual world alongside one another. As we've discussed numerous times thus far, modern VR delivers an immersive experience that you have to try to fully appreciate. It's unlike anything else on the market, and there's no question that it meets its goal of making you feel like you're really there in the world it has created for you.1

The metaverse is the future. It's where all of our devices are headed. Virtual reality can completely transport us to a brand new space, which is something many are looking forward to. You can rest assured that the company you work for certainly is. But what does this mean for other applications? We know work is going to be a significant part of the metaverse's primary uses. We also know gaming will have its place in the metaverse. And we've discussed the applications of virtual reality that transcend medicine and the military, so it's likely that those uses will transition to the metaverse at some point. The future of the metaverse is limitless in terms of what it can be used for. You could go to a virtual college class, meet up with friends, or even visit family in another country. All you need is an internet connection, a VR headset, and a metaverse/Facebook account.

Some companies are already using this technology for training purposes. For example, at Boeing, engineers are using VR to train astronauts. And Stanford University is using it to conduct its classes. But there are many other ways the metaverse could change our lives for the better if we embrace it today. The potential uses of the metaverse are vast and exciting. New businesses will have an easier time advertising their services because virtual spaces are three-dimensional. Companies can create ads on billboards or skyscrapers in 3D worlds instead of in real life. This practice will certainly be a more cost-effective way to advertise to the masses. How marketing will work in the metaverse remains to be seen.

There will almost assuredly be some kind of tax or fee that corporations pay to advertise their goods and services in the metaverse. And when you stop to think of the unlimited space within the metaverse, that's a lot of room for ads.

Hopefully, Meta places tighter restrictions on the way advertising is handled and allowed in the metaverse. Those who remember the early days of the internet can likely recall the mess of pop-ups and ads that permeated some websites. Oftentimes, it was a major chore to search for something online due to all of the unwanted forced ads. In the early days, we didn't have the kind of protection that we have today. No, ads would severely limit your browsing experience, with some dubious websites going so far as to run scripts that tried to automatically install programs on your system.

Thankfully, those days are long gone. But with the infancy of the metaverse, could we see a repeat of these practices all over again? One thing's for certain: if there aren't strict controls to manage these things, companies will try to shove as many ads and content onto you as they can, with reckless abandon. You would think, after all these years, that brands would have caught on and realized that type of "marketing" only serves to push consumers away. And yet, we still see it today. Perhaps that's another story for another time, but you understand the concern. If Zuckerberg and crew have a concrete plan in place to combat wanton advertising, the metaverse can be the utopia it's meant to be. Otherwise, users will quickly get fed up with the invasive marketing techniques that some out-of-touch companies employ.

It's understandable that organizations and enterprises will want to use this new untapped space for personal gain. But the metaverse's potential far exceeds ads and commercials. Let's hope it has the chance it needs to spread its wings and leaves room for more beneficial uses.

A New Way of Life: Working and Living in the Metaverse

No longer will you have to commute in traffic just to get to work. Instead, you could do the morning rush in seconds, essentially teleporting yourself to work. You'll be able to work anywhere— in coffee shops, on planes, or at home. Even from your bed! Or maybe you'll be able to take your virtual dog for a walk in virtual reality. (Not that this will do the real dog much good!) You'll also be able to connect with anyone from all over the world instantly. It'll be easier than ever before to make new friends and collaborate with people from all around the globe—no matter what language they speak or where they live. The metaverse makes this kind of lifestyle possible and will transform life as we know it.

This brings up a lot of myths and misinformation about the metaverse. With the rise of VR, it's no wonder that everyone is curious about the metaverse. But many people still believe that digital worlds are just for gamers. As we've already covered, the metaverse is designed to accommodate many different lifestyles, and that includes both work and play. What are the myths you might have heard about working in these virtual spaces? As it turns out, there are some commonly held myths that simply aren't true.

Some people think you need to be a programmer or have programming skills to use the metaverse. While there are many roles in the metaverse where you certainly could need programming knowledge, the average user does not need any programming skills to enjoy the metaverse and its VR universe. The only time you need specific skills is if your job dictates that you must have them. Otherwise, only a basic understanding of how to log in and use the metaverse's proprietary interface is necessary.

You can be an artist or designer or even a social media manager in the metaverse. Your job role boils down to what you do in the real world. And if your employer allows you to access your job role via the metaverse and work from home, you will have the freedom to do so. VR and the metaverse will eventually merge many different professions into its digital realm. Right now, we know that VR alone has many applications, such as healthcare, education2, and engineering design. If your current job title doesn't seem like it would be compatible with the metaverse, just wait. It's very likely that as the metaverse grows in popularity and businesses see the worth of switching over to the VR world, that many other professions will eventually adapt.3

While the metaverse is still in its infancy, there are likely many businesses that are wary of opening themselves up to the world through virtual reality. They worry that their data will be exposed and made vulnerable to hackers, but there are solutions for protecting your data. In just about every business, data security is an important consideration. And it's equally important when designing a virtual world for clients to interact with and explore. Given Facebook's robust security, the metaverse will undoubtedly offer ways to protect your data and keep it safe from prying eyes.

But work is only one aspect of life in the metaverse. There's also the concept of living in the metaverse. Companies and individuals alike are already planning out their real estate needs in the metaverse. In a virtual realm, is it really right to sell "land" to people? If you're a business owner, you shouldn't have to worry about location, as your store could theoretically be everywhere all at once. Just like the internet currently, you could see customers from all over the world visiting your store at any given time.

For better or worse, there is talk taking place right now about selling metaverse real estate. In December 2021, one user spent $450,000 to "buy land" in the metaverse. But this wasn't just any land, as it was "next" to the metaverse "home" of Snoop Dogg. You're seeing a lot of quotes used because virtual realms are endless by design. It feels extremely unethical for a need to buy virtual space. It remains to be seen how corporations intend to own and divide land that technically doesn't exist. But if they can make money, you can bet your last dollar that's exactly what they'll do. If you needed further evidence that the metaverse will be a money-making machine for big business, this is it.

And as we've seen, people will spend money on just about anything these days—even if it's nearly half a million dollars to live next to a digital cartoon. Not to be outdone, one firm spent a staggering $4.3 million on "land" in Atari's metaverse, *The Sandbox*.4 With the future of real estate in flux, it's hard to know if we're living in a world with an abundance of housing for everyone or a world where there will be few properties and skyrocketing prices. However, one thing that's certain is that the way we buy and sell homes is changing drastically—the aforementioned purchases verify as much.

In the real world, more and more it seems like property is a luxury for some and reserved for those with the best credit. In the digital world, things should be different. Unfortunately, we're already seeing users and corporations buy up digital land space. The metaverse isn't even here yet, and already we're seeing its potential to make the rich richer. If everyone will be required to hand over their hard-earned money just to thrive in the metaverse, it could quickly turn into a land built solely for the elite.

This could leave many people and some businesses "stuck" in the real world. As we've seen with the internet, if a company hopes to be successful, it must have an online presence. Hopefully, this isn't the case with standard living in the metaverse. When it comes to buying property in the metaverse, you'll need to know how it works before you can dive in. But that means understanding the state of the housing market in the real world, too.

Could we all end up living in shabby pods like in *Ready Player One*, only getting enjoyment from life in a virtual environment? It's a sobering thought, to be sure. Based on the investments we're seeing take place now, it's looking more and more like the metaverse will be the primary point of focus for many people and businesses. On one hand, the metaverse can undoubtedly offer new and beneficial comforts, many of which we've already touched on.

But on the other hand, if major corporations and wealthy individuals are making investments that the average Joe couldn't dream of, what's the point? Who is the metaverse really for? Until we get more information and see the metaverse for ourselves, much is still up in the air. The hope, of course, is that everyone will have a level playing field in the metaverse. Ideally, it should be a realm where anyone can get ahead. It's a completely new world, after all. It's safe to assume that having a clean slate and a fresh start in the metaverse could do wonders for many people. The possibilities are certainly appealing. Hopefully, everyone has a chance to take advantage of those possibilities without prejudice or preference. That includes job opportunities, education, and real estate.

Conclusion

The purpose of the metaverse is to create a safe and accessible space for everyone to connect, transact, and share ideas. Moreover, the metaverse will become the global network of virtual universes that are interconnected. As such, the possibilities for its uses have the potential to be limitless.

In the metaverse, we will converse with doctors, attend sporting events with friends and family, go on dates, watch movies, and more. And because there are so many different roles being played out in the metaverse, the job titles that we'll see will be equally limitless. Some real-world jobs won't be compatible with the metaverse, but a substantial portion of them already are. And those that don't currently fit in the metaverse's mold are likely to adapt as corporations realize the true potential of this new reality.

But it won't be all work in the metaverse. Some users will never work a day in the metaverse, instead using it purely for leisure. Others will find the metaverse to be the ideal setting for exercising and getting into shape. While it might not seem feasible now, there are already fitness applications that work with VR to provide users with an alternative to going to the gym.

Chapter 9

GETTING STARTED: METAVERSE 101

The metaverse is a compelling vision of the future, and one that is becoming more and more like reality with every passing day. VR technology is just getting to the point where it's possible to create a viable environment for multiple purposes. And with the innovation of augmented reality, we are now living in an era where reality and virtual reality are becoming blurred.

The metaverse can be defined as a collection of interconnected universes that exist across various media platforms—most notably, AR and VR. This means that users can enter into diverse worlds through their VR headsets and interact with others within those worlds. The development of the metaverse will change how we perceive both space and time, redefining human existence as we know it. But what do you need to do in order to get started in this virtual realm?

Remember, the metaverse is a world of virtual reality. It's a world where you can be anyone or anything. You can fly, swim, and meet new people. It's our world of imagination come to life. But how do you get there? Since the metaverse is a shared virtual space, it is developed by the collaboration of different realities. It has been developed using 3D computer graphics and 3D displays—virtual reality headsets like the Oculus Rift or Microsoft HoloLens. The people who inhabit this space are represented as avatars. Avatar is a word that refers to an individual's representation of themselves on the internet.

Once you acquire a VR headset and get signed into the metaverse, you will need to customize your avatar to show other users how you want to be seen. Setting up your software and hardware might sound tricky, but it's not too difficult. Let's take a look at what you need to get started.

The Right Equipment

You're going to need the right gear to use the metaverse, as it effectively ditches the days of monitors, mice, and keyboards. Your most essential tech will be your VR headset and a powerful computer. Let's find out what you'll need and how it works to connect you to the metaverse.

A VR Headset: As mentioned earlier in the book, you'll need a VR headset. Some headsets are expensive, while others are cheap, so you'll want to do some research before making a purchase. Right now, the Oculus (Meta) Quest 2 is the gold standard for accessing the metaverse. After the Oculus Quest 2, stands the PlayStation VR, then, the Valve Index. But that doesn't mean other VR headsets won't work with the metaverse. Models such as the HP Reverb G2, LONGLU VR, Pimax Vision Super 5K, HTC Vive Pro Focus Plus, Valve Index VR HMD, and others are already approved for use.

The demand for VR headsets has increased over the last few years, which has helped to get prices to where more of the population can afford these fancy units. There have been many manufacturers enter the VR race, providing budget-friendly options for those who can't or don't want to sink hundreds of dollars into a headset. This, of course, has only served to increase the want for the technology even further. But thanks to all the buzz going around about the impending metaverse, we're likely going to see a slew of VR models hit the market in the near future. Even the mighty Apple is said to be joining the VR race if that tells you how big the metaverse is projected to be.

So, if you're ready to go all-out and spend a sizable chunk of change of the metaverse, your best bet is the Oculus Quest 2. These VR goggles are lightweight and can adapt to your head size with ease. They also have next-generation graphics and a fast processor. You can use these multi-purpose devices for everything from browsing the internet, to completing work-related tasks, to playing the latest video games. And it's very much in the same vein as using smartphones and laptops.

They combine 6GB RAM with the Qualcomm Snapdragon XR2 platform for smooth performance. You're also treated to a resolution of 1832x1920 pixels per eye. The simplest 128GB version costs $299. Controllers are sold separately, and you get one per hand. But they are lightweight and can be adjusted to fit the size of your hands. These buttons are necessary, because you choose the game options using the buttons. They also give you the illusion that your virtual hands and fingers are synchronized. The Oculus Quest 2 glasses, Oculus platform software, and app store are included in your purchase, along with customer service. It costs $799 (the 259 GB version) if purchased through a corporate account.

A Powerful Computer: A good computer is needed to run the 3D worlds created for the metaverse. So, it's likely that many people will need to upgrade or invest in an entirely new system if they want to be able to access the metaverse. This is to be expected, as this new technology is unlike anything we've ever seen. You will definitely want to do your homework on which computer is right for you.

At present, we know that many VR applications require graphics cards of certain capabilities. This means that if you buy a new system, you may need to upgrade the graphics card inside to be able to take full advantage of your VR headset and the metaverse. The VR headset you choose may not be as essential as the computer that's running the software.

Software: With the right software, you can enter the metaverse to enjoy front row seats at your favorite concert, sporting event, or comedy club. Go to concerts on *Beat Saber* and see artists like Billie Eilish and Imagine Dragons. Enjoy live front row seats at an NBA game.

For the working person, *Quest for Business* allows businesses to create immersive virtual reality experiences through Facebook. You can use the business account to work in *Horizon Workrooms* or *Gravity Sketch* to create 3D models. The beta version, which became available to select companies in 2018, is still experimental. It will be available to all companies beginning in 2023. Moreover, Slack, Dropbox, and Canva are all coming soon to VR as 2D panel apps in *Horizon*. You can easily update files and tasks without having to take your headphones off.

A Metaverse App: The other piece of software you need is an app to download onto your device or computer to view the content of the metaverse. While there will likely be many apps to choose from eventually, the metaverse is the one that everyone is talking about. And it's likely to set the standard for what a VR realm should be. Once the metaverse launches at large, it's only natural that other companies will release their own VR worlds. In fact, some already have limited virtual realms for users to explore. But to access the metaverse, you will need to download its accompanying software to get started.

After downloading the correct software and setting up everything correctly, it's time to start navigating the metaverse. Once you've set up your software and hardware and logged in, you're free to explore the virtual world before you. You may already be familiar with social media platforms like Facebook or Twitter. But in the metaverse, you can go even further than what you could do on those platforms.

One of the most common things people do in the metaverse is socialize. You can meet new people and talk to them just like you would in real life. The only difference is that they aren't physically there with you. One of the best ways to meet people is through a chatroom. There will likely be many different chatrooms for all sorts of interests, from sharing your opinion on current events to discussing anime. You can also make friends who share your interests and passions by visiting their homes or places they want to show off.

For many people out there, social media has become a major part of their daily lives. Whether it be Facebook, Twitter, or Instagram, these sites are always buzzing with activity. One of the best parts about these platforms is that you can constantly see what your friends are up to. But there is a downside to this. Many users feel less compelled to check up on friends and family because they feel like they're always connected to them. But this is a façade. The fact of the matter is that many people neglect making contact.

But social media has other drawbacks, too. Chief among them, it can decrease your productivity. It's easy to get distracted by checking social media sites when you should be working or studying instead. When someone posts a new photo on Facebook or tweets something, it's easy to stop what you're doing to see what they posted (this plays into the false sense of connection). But with virtual reality, if someone posts something it will pop up in front of your face and you can decide whether or not you want to look at it. And since VR is more immersive than scrolling through your newsfeed, chances are that this person will have more of an impact on your life because of the increased time spent with them.

Another downside is that social media might cause envy among friends who appear happier than you are. Social media sites are great for sharing photos and videos with friends, but some people may feel jealous of others who have more followers or seem to have a more exciting life. This envy may lead some users to feel left out and disconnected from their friends on these sites. Finally, there's the issue of privacy concerns on these sites. Many people use their real names instead of aliases, which means that anyone can find out everything about them just by typing in their name into Google search or looking them up on Facebook. With VR and the metaverse, there's a greater level of anonymity, if that's what you prefer.

The metaverse aims to fix many of the current issues with social media. While virtual reality allows you to meet new people while still being able to stay in touch with your old ones on social media, it also means that you can feel more connected with people who live far away from you without having to spend tons of money on travel. And since the immersiveness and interactivity of the metaverse is leaps and bounds ahead of current social media, you will want to connect with your friends and family.

Furthermore, the metaverse allows you to experience things that you might never otherwise have the chance to do while still being able to stay in touch with your friends and family on social media. For example, while you're at work all day, your kids are at school. With VR, they can still have a face-to-face conversation with you while they do their homework or play at recess. But beyond increased opportunities for communication, VR has so many other benefits, as well. You can travel anywhere in the world without worrying about how far or expensive it is because the cost of traveling virtually is nothing. Plus, there are so many other people who are doing exactly what you are doing—exploring new worlds and meeting other people from around the globe.

All of this is made possible with the metaverse. Once you're active in the virtual environment, you can see and do just about anything your heart desires. This sense of exploration gives users an experience that just isn't possible with traditional social media and the internet. You'll actually want to meet new people in the metaverse, something that isn't very appealing in the current state of the internet. Indeed, it can be really difficult to meet new people—especially if you don't have an active social life.

But as long as you have a headset and a computer, it's easy to find people to hang out with in the metaverse. Moreover, there will be tons of apps that allow you to chat and meet up with other users. And as more users enjoy the metaverse, the more apps you'll see become available for it. Far beyond basic meet and chat functions, you will see a cavalcade of new and exciting apps designed to take full advantage of the VR and AR possibilities of the metaverse.

As for what this means for you, virtual reality and the metaverse provide you with an immersive experience unlike anything else. You can use these technologies to do many things, including playing video games, taking online classes, exploring vast 3D spaces, meeting new people, working, and more.

Conclusion

As we've learned thus far, the metaverse is a virtual reality-based form of the internet and Facebook that will be accessed through headsets and other devices. There will be a whole new dimension of the internet—one that we can experience and explore with our own bodies.

erMASTER THE METAVERSE**   **WES BERRY**

As such, the first step to getting started in the metaverse is understanding what it is and how it will change your life. The second step is preparing for it by investing in some equipment now so you're ready when it arrives. As you might expect, there are plenty of prerequisites for being able to explore the universe that Zuckerberg build. You need a virtual reality headset, which will allow you to see the world around you as you explore this entirely new dimension. And if you want to have any input into your exploration, you'll need a motion controller, which enables you to interact with objects in this virtual world. Oh, and you'll need a Facebook account.

But that's only the technical side of things. You will also need to create your avatar; your digital, virtual representation of your real-life self. The avatar creation portion of setting up your metaverse profile is sure to be a significant part of the metaverse, as it lets you convey yourself to other users in ways not possible in the real world.

153

Chapter 10

CHOOSE YOUR AVATAR

Get this. You spend more time in the digital world in a day than you do in your actual physical vicinity. In our everyday social life, we often stress what to wear and how to align our fashion and outfits in the best way possible. Then why not do it in the metaverse?

Since metaverse is the digital, more-advanced representation of the world around us, there is no reason for us not to look the part when we are a part of the system! We can do this by making our avatar dress and accessorize according to the different virtual situations.

Before we dive into how to choose and dress your avatar, it is crucial to understand the term's nuances. The word 'avatar' originates from Hinduism and its serene mythology. It loosely translates to the descent of a deity in terrestrial form. Now, you must wonder how a term related to mythology became so prevalent in the metaverse?

Here's your answer.

In 1985, a video game programmer named Richard Garriott referred to his virtual player as an 'avatar'. He wanted to make his virtual character a proper digital impersonation of his real-life personality. The term spread like wildfire throughout the whole gaming industry and is now used famously in prominent games like Nintendo Wii to the James Cameron larger than like film *Avatar*.

Since your avatar is supposed to be a digital photocopy of your real-world personality, it is essential to ensure that their style aligns with yours. Since metaverse is a whole different world, you can say that your metaverse avatar is literally *you* in the digital sense.

Why do you need to put so much stress on your avatar's appearance? I have an answer to this, and it's called 'The Proteus Effect.'

The Proteus Effect states that our performance in the metaverse is affected by the features of our avatar. The two prominent researchers of this effect, Jeremy Bailenson and Nick Yee, claim that the virtual character's appearance and height influence their performance.

In the research, they found out that players with more attractive characters were more pro-efficient and open with other players. Meaning, the two attractive characters stood closer to each other and talked about themselves.

Secondly, they found out that participants with taller avatars performed significantly better than other players in tasks that evolved negotiations. Overall, they exhibited assertive and dominant personalities.

This is the reason why entities in the metaverse are coming up with new ways every day to provide you with the option of personalizing your avatar as much as possible.

Some games provide you with the option of a literal embodiment of yourself into your avatar. All you need to do is upload a headshot photo or simply use your webcam to trace your face into the game's database.

Once this is done, the technology automatically traces down different angles of your face and embodies them into your avatar. However, you must keep in mind that several factors like light, color, and the quality of the image might affect the final outcome of your avatar.

Now that we know how much importance our avatar can hold in the metaverse, it's time to dial down on how to choose the best character for yourself and make them dress the part.

Let's get started.

Dress For The Occasion

In research conducted over the years, it was found out that people's clothing directly affects their work performance. For example, a sports jersey can make an athlete feel at ease and make him perform better. Candidates who wear formal clothes to interviews stand a better chance of grabbing the job, and so on.

When we turn our eyes to the digital space, this effect is magnified. In the online world, the avatar is not only the costumes that it wears, but it is the entire self-representation of the player. Therefore, it is empirical to make sure that your character has his outfit game on point for you to perform at your optimum level in the metaverse.

The fact that your avatar is customizable at all times in most of the games leaves you with no excuse to not make them look the best they can. However, the whole act of shopping and fashion works slightly differently in the metaverse as compared to the conventional paradigm.

Let's look at how styling works in the 'verse and how it can say a lot about you.

What are Digital Clothes?

Grasp your head around everything that you can associate with clothes, the colors, cloth, size, cuts, and put them into the digital set-up. That's what digital clothing is. Digital garments are not made of fabric. They are made of pixels using technology and 3D design.

As far as the metaverse is concerned, clothing your avatar is one of the most satisfying parts of many games.

How To Buy Clothes For Your Metaverse Avatar

As metaverse continues to soar in popularity, more and more brands are investing their time and money into the prospect of digital clothing. This means that you have no shortage of options when it comes to buying dope outfits for your avatar.

Adidas recently announced that they are about to launch a new collection that will be available both digitally and in reality at the same time. This means that your avatar in the metaverse can have the same sneakers that you wear to your parties.

Clothing brand H&M is coming up with the prospect of offering a three-dimensional shopping experience in the metaverse for your avatar. They are planning to name this digital shopping center CEEK City Universe.

Some other brands taking long strides in the metaverse fashion include Gucci, Louis Vuitton and Balenciaga.

How To Pay?

You can pay for your avatar's outfit with the help of non-fungible tokens in the metaverse. The blockchain application stores the record of all such transactions.

Payments are made with the help of cryptocurrencies, with new options coming in every day. If you are wary of the volatility of these coins, you'll be pleased to know that more stable coins are being introduced into the metaverse to provide for more seamless transactions.

Dress According To The Role

Alright, now that you know how to buy clothes in the metaverse, it is time to dial down on what to buy. Just like in real life, your outfit can change completely depending upon the kind of work or the type of setting you're going to.

If you're going for a virtual party in the metaverse, get your avatar an outfit with some jazz and finesse. There are zillions of options to choose from, right from Balenciaga to the emerging British brand Stefan Cooke.1

On the flip side, if you are just planning to walk in the streets, putting on a hoodie can be the ideal choice. However, make sure that your outfit is not completely basic since metaverse is your ticket to release yourself from physical realities. Unleash your creativity and push the limits.

The internet provides you with the opportunity to express yourself. Clothing can be an excellent instrument for doing that. Things move fast around the metaverse. Therefore, to make sure you and your avatar stand out, you need to find the perfect skins and costumes.

Dress up and make the most of the fashion conglomerate present in the 'verse and let your avatar speak for itself.

Metaverse Collaborations

The metaverse provides an excellent platform for both brands and users to experiment with their styling. Several brands have resorted to the gaming industry to bring a new chapter to their marketing.

Here is a list of the most celebrated clothing and gaming industry collaboration:

1. Gucci X Roblox

   In May 2021, the game Roblox pulled of something called The Gucci Garden. It was a two-week art installation program aimed at raising brand awareness with customers.

   It was a digital world re-creation of the real-world event that took place in Florence. Just like its real-life counterpart, the Gucci art show offered various theme-based rooms to pay tribute to the brand's campaigns.

   After entering the digital area, players could try on and purchase digital Gucci clothing to dress their avatars and then walk through the themed doors. The experience was primarily designed to raise awareness of Gucci's digital item launch on the game Roblox.

2. Louis Vuitton and Louis The Game

   In 2021, Louis Vuitton celebrated its second centenary by launching the adventure-based game - *Louis The Game*.

   The game follows the journey of Vivienne, the company's house mascot. The primary mission is to collect 200 candles to celebrate the birthday of Louis Vuitton. The game featured exclusive digital skins provided by the brand itself.

3. Balenciaga and Fortnite

   This was probably one of the most celebrated metaverse milestones of all time. When Balenciaga partnered up with *Fortnite* to enter the metaverse, the world was left in awe. Players of the game could purchase digital outfits that were inspired by real-life Balenciaga clothing. Most of the costumes had to be bought, except the Triple S sneakers that could be unlocked.

4. Selfridges and Pokémon

   2021 marked the completion of 25 years of Pokémon. To celebrate that, Selfridges, in collaboration with designer Charli Cohen and Yaho Ryot Lab, developed Electric City.

It was a digital shopping center where you could buy exclusive virtual products.

Don't Forget Hair and Makeup

If you thought that the fashion around the metaverse was only restricted to clothing and footwear, then you're about to get surprised.

With the beauty industry slowly finding its footing in the 'verse, our virtual avatars have the option of embracing the most cutting-edge makeup routines.

Makeup might not be the first thing that comes to your mind when you think of the gaming industry. However, in recent times, the gaming world is breaking free from its gender stereotypes, making beauty brands understand the promotional capacity of the metaverse.

At a time when men and women around the world are refraining from makeup in their real-life unless they have to go out, you can use your virtual avatars as means of expressing your boldness. Beauty brands who are looking to enter the metaverse need to be customizable with their marketing, patient with the players' response, and accepting of different options. The adoption of makeup in the metaverse can be as small as using an AR filter.

However, as some games have already shown, the scope of growth in the 'verse is magnificent.

We'll be looking at some metaverse entities and their relationship with the beauty industry shortly, in the next segment.

Beauty brands are slowly realizing that gaming is far more mainstream than many people realize, especially among women. If you think that only teenagers and young adults are interested in the metaverse concept, you are highly mistaken. According to a Global World Index research, 53% of beauty enthusiasts played or downloaded a free game.2 Therefore, in all possibilities, the metaverse is a vast untapped market for the beauty industry.

You can change just about anything you like in the metaverse. And you can do it in an instant. Different games provide different scopes and choices for making your avatar stand out.

Select hairstyles, makeup, accessories, and more to experiment with your character as much as you want. However, keep in mind that all this stuff will cost you!

Some Games Offering Hairstyles and Makeups

There is no denying the fact that makeup and other parts of the beauty industry haven't shown their full effect on the metaverse yet. However, some specific games allow you to experiment with different hairstyles and makeup trends for your avatar.

Let's take a look at some of them.

1. Zepeto

    It is a South Korean metaverse launched by Never Z Corp that has partnered up with brands like Nars, which offers several makeup looks, and Dior Beaute, which provides exclusive looks created by Peter Philips.

    Something like this is more than enough to lure a beauty enthusiast into the metaverse. This opens up a plethora of beauty options for players to get creative and develop new designs from the options available.

2. Fortnite

    The frontrunner of online games, *Fortnite* provides many options for customizing the hairstyle and skins of your avatars. It hasn't partnered up with any beauty brand as of yet, but the game already has some fascinating in-built options to choose from.

The options for hairstyle, makeup, and other beauty accessories are expected to grow in the near future in the metaverse. With the right match of costume and style, you can make your virtual self stand out from the crowd.

Conclusion

If you get a kick out of creating characters in video games, you're going to love the metaverse's avatar creation tool. It's here that you will be able to make your virtual self look any way you desire. You can choose which hairstyle you want to wear to work, what shirt to carry for a party, apply makeup for a date, buy new shoes to exercise in, and so much more.

The metaverse has no boundaries. You can express yourself to the fullest with the help of an online character. The creative possibilities are endless, and you can bet that big corporations are already dreaming up ways to charge you for their in-metaverse products.

Want to carry a Gucci handbag around the metaverse's shopping malls? Or maybe you want the latest pair of Jordans to show off to your friends. It's all possible in the metaverse. You can look however you want, from your clothing to your eye color. With the fashion giants like Nike and Balenciaga already investing in this digital fashion world, one can say that it can well become the new marketing hub for other major companies. This means that you'll never run out of quality options for styling your avatar.

What's more, you don't even have to present yourself as a human if you don't want to. Perhaps you'd feel more comfortable as a shark or an android. The metaverse lets you do that and more. But this stuff isn't going to be free. While it's likely that you can create a generic avatar of yourself to get started, anything beyond that is going to cost you real-world money. But how exactly will that work in the metaverse? Let's take a look.

Chapter 11

HOW WORK WORKS

The future of work is the subject of many conversations. We've seen time and time again where new technologies go on to shape how we work, play, and make money. Some people might not like it, but the world of work is evolving, and it's doing so at breakneck speeds. And if you're an employer or an employee, it's important to stay on top of these changes. It may be hard to imagine, but if you think back to just a few decades ago when working meant sitting in a cubicle all day at a large company with a very structured 9-to-5 schedule, it's easy to see that the world has changed in many ways.

Without a doubt, technology has reshaped our lives in very significant ways and in every aspect. And with the advent of the metaverse, things are about to change yet again. So what will your day in the metaverse look like? What are some ways to prepare for this future?

The future of work is changing. Technology alone has exponentially changed the way we work. It's made it easier to work remotely, and it's given us tools that help us do our jobs with more efficiency and less physical effort. And as the world of work changes, we must embrace these changes with forward-thinking strategies and progressive adjustments. One way is to offer remote positions or telecommute opportunities for employees. This will allow more people to choose when they want to work, where they want to work, and how they want to work, all while getting their essential tasks completed in an efficient and controlled manner.

> *Businesses and enterprises are learning the hard way that they can either resist the impending change or embrace it.*

Another is to offer flexible schedules for employees. For example, if an employee wants to take a few days off during the week or work four 10-hour days instead of five 8-hour days, that is completely possible and should be allowed by various employers. Or, if an employee needs a break in the middle of the day for a doctor's visit or any other individual circumstance, they should have the ability to take those breaks without losing their job. While this wasn't really possible when working those cubicle-confined jobs of yesteryear, it's more than feasible thanks to the freedom of today's remote landscape.

Life in the metaverse is all about alternatives. In it, you can choose to live an alternate lifestyle, and that includes work if your employer allows it. As we've already touched on, many companies have embraced remote working in light of the pandemic. It's a radical shift, to be sure. But it's one that has opened the door to many new possibilities and benefits for those companies that can look past the trees and see the forest.

Many businesses and enterprises are learning the hard way that they can either resist the impending change or embrace it. One way to prepare for change in the future of work is to be open to trying new things. Those companies that have embraced remote work will likely embrace a metaverse lifestyle, as well. From advertising opportunities to high morale, there's a lot to be gained from doing business in the metaverse. And unfortunately, many companies will get left behind for not adopting the metaverse lifestyle sooner.

Whether you are an employee or an employer, resisting change will only hurt your business endeavors in the long run. A few ways to embrace change are through employee education, investing in new technologies, and having a positive attitude about change.

Education will help employees understand how changes are affecting their jobs and how they can adapt accordingly. Investing in new technologies will mean that businesses will have the resources needed to keep up with evolving trends. Lastly, embracing change with a positive attitude will help employees better adjust to shifts in the way they work. It's important for everyone involved with the company—employees included—to have an understanding of what these changes are doing so that they can come up with strategies on how to best use them for their benefit.

A Job Well Done

It's undeniable that the workforce is changing faster than ever before, and the workplace is becoming more and more virtual. The technology that used to be too expensive, too bulky, or just not good enough has evolved into an entire industry of products that offer affordable, accessible solutions for businesses and individuals alike.

The introduction of virtual reality into our lives has also changed the conversation. Virtual reality is an immersive experience and with all its possibilities, it may very well be the future of employment. With VR technologies advancing ahead of their time, you can bet there will be plenty of opportunities for entrepreneurs to capitalize on this industry, as well as those who are looking for a career change. But as we just discussed, many workers may not have a choice.

If you're a business owner, consider for a moment the advantages that moving your storefront to a virtual space presents. VR allows your customers to explore your store virtually, go on a virtual tour of your business, or even learn about new products at your company's stand at the event of their choosing. A virtual reality headset can also allow you to walk through building plans with clients and present new ideas in a collaborative environment.

VR and AR technologies are quickly revolutionizing the way we do business, and they're likely to forever alter the way your business operates. The immersive environments of the metaverse certainly make the prospect of doing business a lot more exciting. While VR is often thought of as something that would take away jobs from workers, there are actually many ways it could help employees do their job better or expand their skill set without leaving the comfort of their office chair. Whether you're looking for a way to take your latest product idea from concept to reality or just want less back pain from sitting too long at your desk, virtual reality and the metaverse could be the answer.

In addition to convenience, businesses that engage in the metaverse will be able to operate across borders and meet potential customers that would otherwise be inaccessible. And it's all thanks to the metaverse and the possibilities it allows. This is a new way to do business. It expands your market and provides an immersive environment where participants can communicate, collaborate, compete, create, and socialize.

For example, let's say you need a web developer for your company. The client you need may not be in the United States or in your country's area code. But with the metaverse, they can be right next door to you or on the other side of the world and you can still work together seamlessly. If this sounds a lot like the current state of ecommerce, it's not too far off. The metaverse and VR business owe a lot to the internet. It set the stage for what's to come. And while you'll still technically need an internet connection to do business in the metaverse, its interface will be an entirely new experience.

It's no secret that the introduction of digital technologies like the internet has made doing business significantly easier. However, it also brings with it a number of challenges. One such challenge is how to maintain customer privacy in an increasingly digital world. As we continue to go further and further into this digital world, we become more vulnerable to sophisticated hacks that could lead to the loss of our personal and business data.

Business owners will need to be well educated about the metaverse. But safety and security don't only apply to major corporations. Workers will also need to take precautions to ensure that they don't fall victim to a cyberattack (meta-attack?).

The metaverse is a new reality, a digital space as detailed as reality, as real as reality. In this world, it is possible to create your own world, your own universe, your own everything. But with that comes the same kinds of risks and threats we see in the modern world. And you can rest assured that there will be those who want to take away what's rightfully yours.

At the same time, it's important not to lose sight of the many benefits that the metaverse presents: easier workflow, increased efficiency, and lower costs. The challenges are just as clear, but with the right approach, you can be sure to get the most from your metaverse experience.

Like anything new, adjusting to life in the metaverse will likely take some time. If you're new to the concept of VR, this is especially true. Many people have already gotten used to the idea of working from home, but there are many more who have either not had the opportunity or outright refused it as being inconceivable. The truth of the matter is that remote work is here to stay, and it's only going to become more prominent as time goes on.

If you find yourself balking at the idea of working in the virtual worlds of the metaverse, there are a number of ways to prepare for this future. The first thing you should do is to be adaptable. It's important to be flexible and open-minded enough to consider what the future may hold. Many companies and workers have already reaped the rewards of choosing to be flexible in this area. And you can, too, as long as you resolve not to stay rooted in your way of thinking.

It's important that employers and employees stay informed and educated about the changes happening with remote work and the metaverse, as it's one of the most important steps to being ready for what's to come. In the years to come, we're likely to see a significant shift in the way businesses operate. If you've not made strides to adapt to this new way of working, you, too, will get left behind.

Employers can help their workforce by educating them on how they might work in the future. And employees should do their research to better prepare themselves for this new era. They should also stay up to date with skills needed for jobs, both emerging and traditional. If you don't know what you will need for a life in the metaverse, you risk becoming irrelevant quickly, and the same holds true for corporations, both large and small. It's important to make sure you area always up to date with what skills you need to maintain success in the rapidly changing world of working in the metaverse.

In doing so, you can ensure that you will easily adjust to any coming changes. One day, your employers might approach you about everyone having to move over to the metaverse platform. You want to be ready to ensure a smooth transition. It's a testament to why it's so important to embrace change, which the metaverse is certain to bring.

Conclusion

If you were one of the fortunate people who didn't get laid off during the pandemic, chances are that you're already familiar with working from home. There's a significant portion of the population who have already cut their teeth on remote work. So, by the time the metaverse launches and companies shift operations to the metaverse, many people will be prepared to jump right into it.

Others, however, may have trouble adjusting to this new way of life. Because as it stands, not every corporation is on board with the metaverse. But as they start to see the value in switching over to the metaverse, these businesses will have no choice but to adapt. Those that don't, run the risk of falling behind the times or even going out of business altogether.

We see the same concept with the internet in today's industries. Just about every company has a website or Facebook business page. The ones that don't can't compete with the power of ecommerce. Will we soon see "metacommerce?"

If all of this sounds overwhelming, it's best to take a step back and start from square one. Let's look at the basics of getting started in the metaverse and what you'll need to get online.

Chapter 12

GET FIT IN THE METAVERSE

Virtual reality is a new way of experiencing the world. With the metaverse set to change the future of entertainment, architecture, and even health care, VR equipment has already begun to make inroads in the fitness and physical therapy industries. With VR and the metaverse, you can use your own body weight and exercises like squats, lunges, planks, and push-ups to improve your physical condition while simulating different terrains like mountains or oceans.

You can also practice yoga or do aerobic workouts while exploring virtual worlds. Have you ever wanted to be a rock climber? Or run with the bulls? Now you can with VR technology. Combined with the vast social construct that is the metaverse, you will be able to exercise in ways that weren't possible until now. Just imagine cycling in the Tour de France alongside Tadej Pogačar—from your living room or basement! That's the revolutionary experiences that are only possible with the metaverse.

While it's certainly possible to use traditional weights, the metaverse opens the door to a whole new realm of physical fitness options. A common problem people face when trying to exercise is a lack of motivation. After all, it's hard to stick with something when you don't see any immediate or short-term benefits. One way the metaverse will help make exercising more enjoyable and maintainable is by giving you instant access to like-minded people around the world who are looking for a workout partner. For example, if you want to run a 10k race but don't have the drive to complete it, your partner can be there to push you to the finish line. You can work together to motivate one another while building a friendship. You'll feel accomplished and stay motivated as you work towards your ultimate goal.

The metaverse is a virtual reality network that has come to be much more than just a gaming platform. It has become a social hub, travel destination, and workspace. With the rise in VR headset sales in recent years, it is evident that the metaverse will continue to grow as an essential part of our digital lives. The best way to take advantage of this new world is by being active in it. But how do you get moving when you're in a digital environment?

Given that most people will be confined to a limited area, some creativity will need to be implemented to get your workout in. While it's true that VR is still relatively new, it's quickly gaining popularity for its ability to make the user feel more present in the virtual world. As such, VR has made exercise fun again with games that simulate various sports, an immersive experience that tricks your brain into thinking you're actually on a long run or cycling up a hill. But that's only one component of exercising in a virtual space. With the simulation part out of the way, users need to think about how they can move in place.

Fortunately, companies are already working out the kinks to make this possible. For example, Omni One has developed a stationary treadmill that VR users stand on, allowing for movement in a singular location. You can run, jump, crouch and crawl—all without leaving the confines of the treadmill. There have been similar products already: the creators of Omni One appear to have figured out how to eliminate accidental straying while in use, a problem that plagued these contraptions in the past. With the Virtuix, Omni One's VR treadmill, users stand in a dish-like structure while strapped in with shoulder harnesses. These harnesses are affixed to a crane that helps support the user's weight while providing balance. This setup allows you to achieve greater physicality while playing games or just walking around town. Thanks to the dish base, you can walk or run in place without leaving the unit. Furthermore, there are tiny casters underneath the base that allow the unit to turn with you, so you can perform 360-degree movements without issue.

Accessories like the Omni One Virtuix are one of those rare exceptions where a third-party device adds true value to the medium it's supporting. But be ready to fork over a pretty penny if you want this VR treadmill in your home. At last report, the Virtuix costs about $2,000. This might sound steep, but if you're serious about your VR experience, the Virtuix is likely a must-have addition to your setup. And thanks to the innovation it brings to the table, users can finally break free from the confines that VR is known for, thereby adding a whole new layer to the metaverse and VR use as a whole.[1]

Catch the Game from Home

Virtual reality has been popular for years, but it's only recently that the tech has gained enough momentum to make VR mainstream. What used to be a tech toy for early adopters is now showing up in many people's homes. And as users will soon discover, services that are similar to *Netflix* will make it possible to watch sports in the metaverse. It's not just about being immersed in live-action, though. The technology also allows viewers to watch sports from any angle, whether they are courtside or in the nosebleed section.

In the past, you might have been limited to watching from TV or from your seats at the stadium. But with VR streaming services, you can watch your favorite sporting event from anywhere in the world. From the comfort of your own home, you can experience the first-person point of view of what it's like to be courtside or on the sidelines at a live event. But where the metaverse takes this experience to the next level is by allowing you to hang out with your best friends at your favorite games. It's like you're really there in person—all while you sit on your couch.

For sports lovers who are looking to stay in the game, the metaverse will introduce you to a whole new take on live sports. By putting on your headset, you can see the game in 3D and in real-time, with 360-degree views. You can finally get a feel for what it's like to be at the game from the comfort of your own home.

Conclusion

It's certainly been interesting to see how many of our everyday activities have changed since the global COVID-19 pandemic. With many people forced to work from home and attend classes and meetings over *Zoom*, it was only a matter of time until people found ways to circumvent their daily exercise routines. It didn't help that many gyms closed down, some permanently. To this day, one of the trending topics in VR is fitness.

How do you stay active when you're not able to go to the gym? VR has the solution. Virtual reality makes it easier to work out because you can exercise for longer periods of time without risking injury or exhaustion. You can also multitask while doing your cardio by reading a book or watching videos. That's what users are capable of doing in the here and now.

Once the metaverse becomes a reality, it will serve as a central hub for all sorts of things, exercise included. You'll be able to meet up with friends and run a 5k (possibly with the help of additional peripherals), attend virtual yoga classes with exercise partners, and much more. And if you think that sounds fun, wait until you go on a date in the metaverse.

Chapter 13

DATING IN THE METAVERSE

Even the current generation is still a bit stymied by online dating. Not that it's any easier or better than dating in real life, but there's something notably different about trying to build a relationship over the internet. Maybe it's the unknown, as you never really know whom you're talking to until you actually meet them. Or perhaps it's the fact that both you and the person on the other end have had your fill with real-world dating. If these things bother you, prepare for them to get a whole lot worse once the metaverse arrives. There's no question that dating in the metaverse will parallel online dating as we currently know it; you'll meet digital representations of prospective dates, find things to chat about, and test the waters to see if there's any chemistry between you and your date.

But what is certain to cause some trepidation is the fact that you never really know who is on the other end. With online dating, all you have to go by is a username and profile picture. But in the metaverse, each user's avatar adds a whole new layer to the matter. It's as if that person is there, in a sense, which can be a double-edged sword in some ways. Is it possible to grow attached to avatars? One has to assume so, as it's possible that users will start to attribute the attractive aspects of conversation to the in-world avatar. This might sound nonsensical initially, but it's certainly possible that will become the norm. But you again have to ask yourself if you can honestly know someone on a personal level without first meeting and spending time with them. Digital voice dictation has become really good in quality, and it's likely that many users will use that in their metaverse interactions.

While these are all valid concerns that every honest user needs to be aware of, there are also positives to consider with dating in the metaverse. By having an on-screen avatar do all the gesturing for you, there's no need to get all dressed up. That means no fancy outfits, no makeup or hairdos, no nice shoes—heck, no need to shower if you don't want to. Remember, your avatar is your digital representation. And as such, it's going to take care of the presentation. All you will need to do is come up with some engaging conversation. Adults who have grown weary of traditional dating will undoubtedly find this aspect of the metaverse appealing. But does it have the potential for love to blossom?

A New Take on Love

It's a fair question to ask: "Can love truly blossom in the metaverse?" Given the fact that people have fallen in love online before, it's safe to assume that will be the case in the metaverse. In fact, the more probable answer is that it will be even easier to fall in love via the metaverse. As we just discussed, there's something tangible about dating in the metaverse that isn't possible with typical online dating. You and your date will be able to go to movies, sporting events, operas, concerts; you name it. You can even hold hands as you whisper sweet nothings in your date's digital ear.

Just recently, Meta announced that it is working on gloves specifically designed for metaverse wear. These gloves come courtesy of Meta's Reality Labs division, a branch that is responsible for research and development. When users don these mitts, they'll be able to "feel" things. When you pick up an object, haptic feedback provides stimulation on your fingertips, thereby emulating touch. But Meta Reality Labs aren't the only ones working on this kind of technology. As mentioned, there are going to be many more companies presenting products designed to enhance the metaverse experience. It's safe to assume that we will soon start seeing other wearable clothing and devices that provide

187

haptic feedback. To what extent remains to be seen. But given the nature of the internet, it doesn't take much imagination to guess what this will lead to.1

Conclusion

The internet has long served as a platform for meeting new people and forming relationships. But the metaverse is poised to take this concept to a whole new level. There's only so much connection you can make with another person via text and emojis. Thanks to the power of the metaverse, you'll be able to look right into your date's eyes, hold their hand, and whisper in their ear.

Not only that, but you'll also be able to attend movies together or cuddle up next to each other—all without either of you ever leaving your homes or physically meeting one another. If you've never tried modern VR, there's something tangible about having the ability to touch and interact with items and people. And given the sheer size and scope of the metaverse's virtual realm, this level of interactivity is sure to change the way we date from here on out.

Add to this the possibility of wearable devices that "enhance" your virtual experience, and you have the recipe for a completely new type of love. But with love comes work. And as we've already discussed, there's going to be plenty of that in the metaverse. If you want to have money to take your love on dates, you'll have to work to get it.

Chapter 14

IS THE METAVERSE NECESSARY?

It wouldn't be wrong to say that the metaverse, since its inception, has promoted hype, confusion, and misinformation. It poses a brilliant prospect. A world where everything aligns to allow you to be whoever you want. A world that enables you to break free from your mundane conventional life. A world that is based on the very idea of providing comfort and excitement to its users. Sure, it sounds fantastic, but the question we are looking to answer in this chapter is, *is it really necessary?*

Do we *really* need the metaverse to move human civilization forward? Is it even logical to think that virtually augmented reality can entirely replicate the world as we know? Do we really need to be a part of the metaverse? These are the questions that this chapter will try to find answers to as we move further along in our journey of understanding the metaverse.

Why Do People Love the Metaverse So Much?

Before we dive into analyzing whether the metaverse is a necessity or not, we need to understand why people love it so much. What makes it stand out from all the other internet revelations that have taken place in the past?

Here are a few reasons why people believe that the metaverse is a big deal.

It Could Be the Internet Everyone Imagines

The metaverse is supported by Web 3.0, which provides it with possibilities that the internet had never seen before. Several tech giants worldwide, including Deloitte, are developing a framework to support the spatial web that is closely linked to the metaverse.

Moreover, Mark Zuckerberg literally referred to the metaverse as 'embodied internet' in his founder's address announcing Facebook's rebrand. This shows that he and his company believe that the metaverse has the scope of literally embodying the whole human experience on the internet, thus, making the internet more immersive than ever. All these developments and announcements point towards the same direction: the metaverse could be the upcoming significant online portal where users from all around the world will engage, buy, sell, and assemble.

> *Our world looks at the viability of every new platform by analyzing its money-making capabilities. The metaverse is no different.*

It has started out as an alternative to social media but has the vision of changing the whole worldwide web as we know it.

Exciting Investment Opportunities

Our world looks at the viability of every new platform by analyzing its money-making capabilities. The metaverse provides yet another source of monetization for content creators and VR developers worldwide, maybe the best that these professions have ever come across.

An economy based on cryptocurrency means less censoring of content and regular royalties. To add to this, several venture capitalists are also interested in getting their hands into the virtual world in its nascent stages and investing in exciting startups. Even if one of these startups booms up, these early investors could dictate the terms of the 'verse for years to come.

By estimates, the metaverse is expected to provide investment opportunities of 1 trillion dollars in terms of advertising, e-commerce, and digital events. To top it all off, you ought to keep the job creation potential of the metaverse. Facebook recently announced it would make 10,000 job openings in Europe itself to build its blueprint for the metaverse.

The 'Work' Is Consistently Moving to the Metaverse

VR adoption for work, collaboration, and education has already increased in the last few years. Companies like Spatial, providing a 3-D alternative to Zoom, are seeing a significant increase in usage. Facebook has even come out with its own offering in this regard called *Oculus for Business.*

As companies continue to grow their expectations from employees in the fast-moving world, VR is expected to be a crucial enabler. It helps workers transform into a hybrid without compromising on the engagement and access of their colleagues.

As Zoom hits its saturation point among users worldwide, AR/VR provides exciting alternatives to enable learning both in the workplace and education institutes. In a recent survey, nearly 2 out of 5 respondents say that they are up for the upcoming VR/AR options for learning.

These are the several exciting upsides that make the metaverse such a promising thing. But what about the downsides? If all the benefits make you feel like there could be nothing with the virtual world, then these drawbacks of the 'verse might help you arrive at a more neutral stance.

What About the Downsides?

The metaverse, just like everything else in this world, comes with its own limitations. Let's take a look at some of them.

Significant Legal and Regulatory Implication

Tech giants are already surrounded by controversies regarding data rights, cybercrime, and user privacy. The metaverse is expected to aggravate this issue.

Currently, the initial Workforce Integrated Performance System (WIPS) of the metaverse provides several exciting options but also comes with its own set of risks. Land rights can pose challenging questions in the metaverse. The regulations of NFTs are constantly under speculation. The concept of so-called extension of your real-life personality—avatars—poses several challenging questions.

As an active internet user, it is extremely difficult to avoid data privacy concerns and threats. The metaverse is only expected to make it worse. Regulatory bodies, organizations, and individual users need to consider this as a severe concern to pre-empt similar or even more significant problems down the line.

The Actual Metaverse Is an Interoperability-leapfrog Away

The most prominent argument for not considering the metaverse as a civilization-changing revelation is that it's several years or decades away from its most actual form.

In a survey conducted in the US, only 36% of respondents said that they are excited for the future that the metaverse holds. Furthermore, the majority of the current working population, meaning people above 30, showed significantly less interest in the concept than the younger generation.

However, a counterargument to this point can be that in his founder letter, Meta's CEO Mark Zuckerberg laid out an expected timeline for the metaverse to kick in. According to it, the first iteration of the 'verse can be available in the year 2023.

All this makes us think about the potentially ugly side of the metaverse.

The Ugly Side

The ugly side of metaverse can be linked to the impending separation between people and reality. It stems from the perspective that makes us think that technology can fully catch all human attention and separate us completely from the real world. There is a strong chance that we become addicted to the metaverse. This can result in our children growing up in a digital environment, ripped apart from the natural essence and cognition of the real world.

We should also throw caution to the fact that this can be an inevitable change in our evolution as human species. Technology is an extension of us and, in turn, an integral part of our future. Even if some people don't agree with the direction in which this civilization is moving, it is inevitably where we are headed.

Some of the potential cons of the metaverse with respect to our public lives can be as follows.

- Make you lose track of time
- Develop an addiction to virtual reality
- Detach you from the real world
- Overstimulate your senses

After analyzing all this, we still need to find the answer to the initial question: Is the metaverse really necessary? Or is just like any other technological paradigm shift like computers were in the 80s, the internet was in the 90s, and smartphones were in 2000, or maybe even cryptocurrencies in the last decade.

Is the Metaverse Inevitable?

In the real world, we have our universe and several other universes. Together, all this is called the multiverse. Similarly, in the virtual world, we can see different universes being created by various apps, games, or simulations, and the whole thing is termed as the metaverse.

Therefore, what we see right now might just be the beginning of several virtual universes that are about to unfold in the near future. But the metaverse is supposed to stretch beyond the vicinities of gaming universes. It is a culmination of augmented, virtual, and physical reality. It is something beyond the universe, derived from 'meta'—a Greek word that loosely translates to beyond.

Okay, so here's an interesting take. There is a theory prevalent in scientists regarding the existence of other civilizations in our universe. A possible answer to the impending question "Why has no other civilization tried to contact us yet" can be that after civilization reaches a given level of evolution, they tend to take refuge in the virtual worlds since the actual universe is too vast and hostile to be approached.

If this is the case, then maybe our civilization is just following an evolutionary pattern through the onset of the metaverse.

How Will the Metaverse Change Your Life?

Top tech trends come and go. Therefore, it is normal for you to wonder whether the metaverse is just another gimmick that will die out with other developments. Currently, we hear plenty of discussion surrounding Facebook's rebranding, Microsoft's Mesh release, and cryptocurrencies like SAND and MANA. But honestly speaking, those are all the implications for high-tech firms or big corporations.

The bigger question still persists: what should you, as an average salary-earner citizen, expect from the rise of the metaverse? Is it actually going to affect your life, or simply remain another headline in the tech section of your favorite magazine? Let's explore all such possibilities and doubts in this section.

Improvement in Self-Expression

When social media became rampant more than a decade ago, some people considered it just another dying-out fad. But for the youth, it emerged as a tool of self-expression. People who faced difficulty sharing their opinions face-to-face gained a platform to share their opinion. We can expect something similar with the metaverse. Here, you can easily stroll around and create your virtual world using the available tools.

You can also check the worlds created by other people or be a prospective viewer. Honestly, the possibilities are endless with the feature of custom-designed avatars and 'new skins.' As a result, you will also meet new people who share your interests, likes, and dislikes.

Media and Entertainment

Are you a sci-fi enthusiast who loves getting teleported to the other universe with your 3-D glasses on? In that case, metaverse also provides you with many entertainment options. You will be able to put on your AR-VR headset and attend virtual concerts, talk shows, watch your favorite sport from the front row, or even tour a theme park.

If you are a budding artist, the metaverse community will also provide you with an opportunity to conduct shows without investing a considerable sum in venue or marketing. Recently, leading artists like Snoop Dogg, Imagine Dragons, BTS, etc., have organized their concerts online. Such possibilities will enable fan communities to knit well together.

You Could Create 'Physical' Locations

We have all created workgroups, shared chats, and spaces to encourage more transparent communication with people in our lives. But is it a solid destination to look forward to? After all, a Facebook or Insta group is just another 2-D space with no actual dimensions. But with the metaverse, you can stop by a coffee shop or meet your friend in the city park.

You could develop a space that works well with your motivation based on your interest. For example, if you plan to run a book club and host occasional readings, what better space than a library? Similarly, you can create virtual offices at your convenience.

Inviting People to Your Imagination

More often than not, people find themselves drowning in a fantasy world. With hyperactive imagination, you could often catch yourself daydreaming. As a result, it is often hard to connect with people in real life. But with the metaverse, you will be able to live out your fantasy. You can pick your dream profession, wear your outfit of choice, and a lot more.

Even entrepreneurs and other business officials can use this platform to host meetings, give virtual tours, and finalize business deals.

More Investment Opportunities

As the current generation is becoming more and more financially literate with time, people are looking for more investment platforms. The metaverse is expected to trigger a bustling economy and bring forward several monetization sources. A decentralized, crypto-based economy will help people invest in virtual real estate, designer clothes, luxurious cars, and a lot more.

The metaverse will also increase real-life job opportunities. For example, Nike has already started recruiting people to create 'Nikeland.'

Why the Metaverse When We Already Have Social Media?

How often have you been surprised by the number of ads you have to scroll through on an average social media platform? More so, you will find that your data is never actually safe, and there's plenty of misinformation spreading via online sources.

But when it comes to the metaverse, there is no telling what will happen in the future. With strict regulations, it can gain much control over what went wrong with social media.

Conclusion

It is normal to wonder about the longevity of the 'Metaverse fad' in today's time. We see plenty of technology developments and trends emerge, only to fade eventually away. After a while, you can expect the same from the metaverse but cannot ignore its real-world implications that are already surfacing. If we really stop considering the current state of the world, we will likely see that it brings a lot of value.

As we observed during the COVID lockdowns, multiple people lost their homes, support systems, jobs, and a lot more. Our world was not prepared to handle the sudden changes, and digital platforms remained the only source of connection to the outside world. The metaverse helps you prepare for unforeseen future circumstances and ensures that people don't lose their jobs. In short, the metaverse presents many opportunities, being the 'escape world' to get away from problems faced in real life.

Along with a significant impact on our economy, the metaverse is sure to impact an individual's well-being. It offers more chances for human interaction and allows people to find their community choice and bond well. Unlike social media, here, you can gather with your group of friends at any physical location, host a concert, or have sleepovers.

Similarly, people in professional settings can work from remote areas and still show up for meetings in the conference room. Sure, it's not the same as being with someone in real life, but it's the next best thing. So, regardless of our feelings on this wild new technology, there's no arguing the fact that the metaverse is a gateway to a safer reality.

Chapter 15

A SAFER WORLD FOR
EVERYONE

Consider this scenario: you put on a set of glasses and are teleported to a gigantic tennis court. Prior to swapping to your professional avatar and entering your virtual workplace for your first meeting at 9:30 AM, you play a few matches.

You decide to try on a few new outfits for lunch you're going to next Saturday, and you end up choosing a shirt you've been coveting for a long time. You're looking forward to finishing work early so you can go to that live concert in Paris. You've done all of this and haven't even left your house.

Doesn't it seem a tad bit presumptuous? Is this anything out of a science fiction film? That's not the case. Welcome to the metaverse, where people live, work, play, and interact in parallel digital realities.

In its fully realized form, the metaverse promises to offer true-to-life sights, sounds, and even smells, where a visit to a Seoul café or a tour of ancient Greece can happen from your home.

The metaverse provides a haven from the perils of everyday life. The world can be a terrifying place with new variants on the upswing, crime on the rise, and ambiguity abound. Luckily, thanks to the metaverse, we don't have to put up with tedium and monotony.

Getting Used to Life in the Metaverse

There will be a perceptible difference in how numerous individuals go about their daily lives as more people find solace in the metaverse. What will this look like, and will there be any ramifications to take note of?

Consider going for a walk down the street. You suddenly remember an item you require. A vending machine surfaces right next to you, stocked with the products and varieties you were contemplating. You come to a halt, select an item from the vending machine, have it delivered to your home, and then resume your journey.

After that, visualize a married couple. The husband offers to take his wife to the supermarket, but she cannot recall the required item's name or type. Her brain-computer interface gadget recognizes it and sends a link to her husband's device, along with information about which shops and rows it is in.

Have we finally reached a significant turning point in our quest for the goal of complete automation? Yes, I believe we have, and the turning point is twofold. For starters, a continuous pandemic has prompted many people to embrace remote work to a greater extent.

Companies such as Facebook are hoping that this will increase offices that use digital avatars and VR technology to form relationships and recover some of the flares that emerge from face-to-face conversations. A slew of additional digital instruments and environments will also strive to increase the speed and quality of remote work.

The other and arguably more exciting trend is a growing demand for digital artifacts like NFTs. To varying degrees, many of us now dwell in a metaverse, and its expanding influence in our lifestyles will be aided by a progressive buildup of virtual worlds and things that establish firm roots in our individual and interpersonal selves.

Distinctive digital assets with seemingly immense financial worth have broken loose from game firms' closed universes and found a home on the web today. The upsurge of the crypto-economic system has resulted in creating new types of collectibles and currency, enabling creatives to commercialize in innovative ways and inspiring individuals to do what they do best: actively seek new ways to increase their financial and social wealth.

The metaverse infiltrates your ordinary life in unique ways based on who you are. Let's suppose you're a recluse who lives in a wooded cabin. For you, life is like a game of Alone. You devote each and every day to ensuring that you have enough food and shelter. You have no interaction with the metaverse.

How about an older adult who was born before the internet gained traction? Perhaps you spend as much time in front of a screen as you do away from it, if not less. You could, however, be a grandma who spends equal amounts of time on growing plants and posting on Facebook.

Your foundational mandate might be a discussion centered on unidentified figures with no physical form. You've enabled a wholly digital thing to become the center of your existence without even realizing it.

Now, take someone like many of us, a geriatric millennial. We used to be really interested in what video games our friends were playing, but we had to be in front of each other to be able to enjoy Nintendo's multiplayer gameplay fully, and we were only concerned about the cartridges that someone possessed, not the costumes that the protagonists wore.

We've even spent money to buy digital cards in games like *Hearthstone*, but their function was to assist our enjoyment of the game, not to serve as a symbol of status to everyone else we encountered online.

Therefore, nobody can argue that our social media standing, or dearth thereof, is not a part of our persona. Even though it takes the form of comments from strangers, we all seek recognition and validation there.

You might think NFTs are a passing fad, yet the worth of digital artifacts has been steadily increasing for years. Teenagers are aware of the profit potential of selling Animal Crossing bells or exchanging virtual broadswords in *World of Warcraft*. Top esports players make six and seven-figure wages. People from all walks of life subscribe for moments on *NBA Top Shot*, allowing them to acquire a GIF.

We may still have trouble believing that a few pixels can be worth a fortune, but the new generation won't hold similar concerns. Virtual items and digital relationships were as important to them as real-world family outings or games right from when they were in primary school.

Adults embrace this mindset as well, whether they see potential or are simply inquisitive about inventing and experimenting. Many individuals in the business and communications industries have delved deeper into the metaverse. They collect and trade numerous NFTs, something they regard as an asset as well as a reflection of one's social standing and demeanor. The NFT market continues to expand in significance.

However, as the metaverse's popularity grows, many people are raising questions about the dangers that could arise in a future where the frontiers between the natural and digital realms continue to fade.

A grandiose picture exists of a system of fully realized virtual worlds in which people interact as credible avatars and undertake their digital lives across IRL, AR, and VR. That isn't how most individuals live nowadays; however, with each successive year, ordinary life is filtered through avatars and virtual worlds.

> *Although online interactions were a lifesaver during a pandemic when meeting others in person was perilous, research suggests that youngsters whose daily lives are driven by their social relationships online are more prone to suffer from depression.*

Adults are terrified of the future their children will inherit. The sooner you enter the metaverse, the more probable it is that it will have a profound and enduring impact on you as you grow older. Although online interactions were a lifesaver during a pandemic, when meeting others in person was perilous, research suggests that youngsters whose daily lives are driven by their social relationships online are more prone to suffer from depression.

A crucial aspect is building trusted ecosystems inside the metaverse's technology. These trustworthy ecosystems will include incorporating structures, regulations, algorithms, policies, and frameworks into software and hardware production schedules to address the various security, privacy, and safety aspects embedded in the technology's DNA.

The way information is shared across digital environments will have to be considered meticulously to maintain privacy. The elimination of prejudices which will contribute to a non-inclusive or malevolent imitation of the physical world is an additional factor to examine as part of the privacy issues of the metaverse's evolution.

Partaking in the metaverse will necessitate the use of synergistic innovative solutions. This necessitates a global, open-box safety validation procedure of the ecosystems' defense against breaches of integrity, confidentiality, and other security features. These reliable networks will aid in the creation of a secure, diverse, and meaningful digital and interactive existence.

Current concerns in the metaverse could be worsened in a variety of ways. To begin with, there is a potential of unwelcome contact in a more invasive multisensory environment, based on how these virtual spaces are controlled.

When someone we don't know or don't want to interact with approaches us on sites like Instagram, Facebook, and others by texting, friending, or otherwise attempting to contact us, their capacity to contact us is primarily confined to text-based communications, photographs, and emojis.

Consider the possibility of an unwelcome person being able to enter someone's virtual environment and "get up close and personal" with that individual in the metaverse. This could lead to undesirable behavior if there are no robust procedures to prevent, report, and respond to this in real-time.

Considering that many firms strive to integrate touch as an extra feeling in an interactive environment, the threat that damages in the metaverse will seem more "real" with haptic technology.

Remember the haptic gloves we discussed earlier, which will offer tactile feedback to deliver a more exact and lifelike sensation to any activity? While this can boost connection and build a stronger sense of authenticity in a virtual world, malicious people can exploit it in ways that aren't entirely understood yet.

Because of the multidimensional character of the ecosystem in which it is transmitted, the negative information that spreads all too rapidly in our modern online lives may transform in the metaverse to more graphical, 3D, and aural unpleasant stuff that seems more invasive and has a higher impact.

The development of digital currencies can frequently exacerbate the spread of inappropriate content and actions online. Children, for instance, are allegedly employing their avatars to offer lap dances in digital strip joints in exchange for the digital money "Robux." As per a report by ActiveFence, cryptocurrency is a popular alternative for individuals acquiring Child Sexual Abuse Material (CSAM) because of its decentralized governance and autonomy from financial institutions, which ensures anonymity.

Given the importance of virtual currencies in the metaverse, the economic rewards and payment mechanisms that encourage the spread of harmful information are likely to grow in magnitude and scope as Web 3.0 evolves.

Many businesses, academics, civil society professionals, and regulators are lobbying for rules and guidelines to make illegal activities in the physical world illegal in online spaces. *Bumble*, for instance, is campaigning to make cyber flashing illegal. "If obscene exposure is a felony on the street, why isn't it on your computer or phone?" its CEO, Whitney Wolfe Herd, has challenged lawmakers.1

Image-based sexual assault, in which private photographs are circulated without an agreement, is illegal in Canada, Germany, Pakistan, India, and England, according to human rights lawyer Akhila Kolisetty. Several countries lack legislation to address new forms of digital exploitation, such as "deep fakes," in which a person's face is placed on a porn film and then shared on social media.

The Australian eSafety Commissioner assists persons who have been subjected to such abuse, but many other nations trail behind in terms of such processes and regulatory powers. The same is true when it comes to protecting children online. "Our culture says we're committed to safeguarding kids in the material realm, but we haven't seen that in the online realm," said Steven J. Grocki, the head of the Australian Justice Department's child exploitation and obscenity unit. A significant element of controlling the metaverse will be revising laws to impose in a virtual environment.2

The methods by which we develop attack strategies on a digital platform are constantly evolving. There is no such thing as a set development process. We should think about how we design the hardware and software components of technologies to include native security considerations to preserve the authenticity of the provided material, the engagements created by users inside the ecosystem, and the overall reliability of the given virtual environment.

There is no single issue to examine here because secrecy, transparency, originality, openness, confidentiality, and reliability must all be addressed. Threats against virtual machines have already been constructed, using open-source platforms such as Valve's OpenVR platform.

Authorities and various other stakeholders should consider human rights from the perspective of augmented and virtual reality. The regulations, implementation and general moderating processes that platforms employ are other vital areas that can be enhanced.

Because this software connects with our brains, AR and VR platforms require definite terms of service for realistic experiences. We can't just extend current social media regulations to the metaverse. This is critical because, in addition to material, platform administration in digital environments must manage behavior.

A responsive and punitive manner of moderating is currently one of the most frequent ways of administration in digital environments. This does not prohibit detriments from happening in the first place, and malicious people are becoming more skilled in matching the line of regulations, so penalties could often be avoided. Discovering methods to encourage positive interactions and incentivize improved conduct could become a significant component of a secure digital future, notably given the rising safety threats in the metaverse.

What offers us optimism is that there appears to be a group of teenagers aware of the dangers and shun a life spent entirely online. The link between online existence and psychiatric problems may not be as strong as recent research suggested.

The pandemic has served as a stark lesson that internet conversations and online games can only go so far in terms of providing social stimulation. I believe we'll see a surge in offline activities once it's safe to congregate again. Simultaneously, the metaverse's key components are being built into a framework.

Conclusion

It will take time for many individuals to adjust to the metaverse's internal dynamics. Understandably, conducting our ordinary routine in a virtual world isn't for everyone. On the other hand, others will leap in with both feet, eager to escape the humdrum of their daily lives.

Many individuals are currently afraid of contracting the latest COVID variant and are avoiding leaving the house. This sort of a thing isn't a problem in the metaverse. Staying connected to the metaverse all day has a lot of advantages. However, it would be a mistake to discount its consequences.

It's anyone's conjecture what the repercussions might be until we have more studies and investigations on extended life in the metaverse. However, considering the adverse reactions some youngsters have had to excessive use of computers, video games, and smartphones, it's vital to take a step back and realize that the metaverse may pose similar or even more significant risks.

It's also reasonable to suppose that specific users will find the metaverse inviting while others will struggle to adjust to life in virtual reality. We must also evaluate the metaverse's potential impact on our civilization as a whole.

Chapter 16

LIFE AFTER THE METAVERSE

It's important to think about what kind of effects the metaverse will have on everyday life. We know that it's difficult for some people to return to normal activities after being exposed to the internet and technology for extended periods of time. And given the fact that the metaverse is a reality unlike anything we've ever seen or witnessed, it begs the question as to whether it's really good for the whole of society.

Is it possible that life will adapt to the metaverse rather than the other way around? And if that happens, we could find it increasingly difficult to return to the real world. Without a doubt, technology is changing the way we live, work, and play. But it's also changing the way our minds work. These days, many people spend more time online than they do offline. As a result, our brains are becoming more like computers. We're experiencing an increase in ADHD diagnoses and anxiety disorders, as well as difficulty with concentration and decision-making skills.

And it's not just adults who suffer from these changes; children are also affected. Studies show that one in ten children meets the criteria for ADHD (Attention Deficit Hyperactivity Disorder) diagnosis or is on medication for it. As our brains become more accustomed to computers, it becomes increasingly difficult to focus on one task at a time, leading to frustration and deteriorating mental health.

As a society, we're finding it harder and harder to disconnect from technology. With our smartphones by our side, we're always connected, meaning that our brains are always on. But how does this change the way our minds work? Well, there are several negative effects of too much technology use. For one, the aforementioned ADHD diagnoses have increased steadily since 2003 while anxiety disorders have also increased in recent years. Additionally, many people find it hard to focus or make decisions because they're constantly bombarded with information.

However, there are steps you can take to regain control of your brain. One tactic is "mindful computing." This technique requires you to be mindful about how much time you spend online each day and how long you spend using different digital devices. When you notice that your mind begins to wander or feel anxious, distract yourself with a physical activity—go for a walk outside, cook something healthy in the kitchen, etc.—to help keep your mind clear and engaged with your surroundings rather than lost in an online world.

If you find yourself constantly being distracted by notifications or crave instant gratification every time you log on to social media or use your phone, try establishing boundaries for yourself; perhaps only allow yourself 30 minutes of social media per day during certain hours of the day. This will help prevent the effects of prolonged exposure to the internet and computers. And while it's good to know how you can "turn off" technology's effects, it's equally important to understand what it's doing to you.

When it comes to computers and the internet, the average person spends over 10 hours a day interacting with digital devices. That's more time than we spend asleep. It's no wonder, then, that society feels more disconnected than ever. We've strayed away from the social constructs that define us, instead trading them for a mess of various constructs—many of which have no basis in reality.

And with more recent ADHD diagnoses, this mental disorder has increased an estimated 4% in just two decades. Again, one in ten children is diagnosed with this disorder at some point in their life. Furthermore, anxiety disorders are on the rise. According to studies, anxiety disorders have also risen dramatically in the last 20 years, at a rate of about 5%. As such, it's clear that our brains are changing, and not for the better.

Other studies have found that technology may be changing our brains in ways we don't fully understand yet, including impacting memory and attention span. Knowing that there is a possibility that our brains are changing outside of the known ADHD and anxiety disorders is a scary thought. We already know that many people suffer from a lack of concentration and decision-making skills.

Digital technologies aren't just changing how we use our minds; they're changing how our brains work structurally, too. Studies show that when people multitask with digital devices, they have a harder time concentrating and making decisions than when they focus on one task at a time without digital distractions. It's difficult to concentrate when you're constantly getting notifications from your social media feed or phone alerts from email, text messages, and the many other methods of communication.

Add VR to the mix, and we could be looking at a recipe for disaster once the metaverse is in every home. Virtual reality has been a thing of the future for many years now. And now that it's finally here, are we really ready for it? Adding a new dimension to our world, it is a great step forward in technology. However, with this new virtual world come dangers that we need to be aware of. These include addiction, the effects on children and teens, and even whether or not it can cause brain damage. It is important to know what you are getting yourself into before jumping headfirst into this brave new world.

The dangers of virtual reality are more than you might think. For example, people can become addicted to virtual reality and spend hours in their headsets. This has been seen with some gamers who may play for hours on end. Some lose track of time, forget to eat, and hold off going to the bathroom. It is not entirely clear if these intense hours of playing and focus on a screen can actually cause damage to the brain or not, but it is something that needs to be evaluated more closely.

Children and teens should be careful, as well, as they may not know the difference between what is real and what is fake. They could become desensitized over time and start to believe that the violence they see in VR is normal. We need to ensure that children and teens understand that there are consequences for their actions in these virtual worlds. If you've ever used modern VR, you're likely aware of how easily it can blur the lines between the real world and the digital world.

If the metaverse lives up to its hype, this blurring of realities will undoubtedly become a widespread concern. And as many children and teens are having their first go at virtual reality, it is important to note that they can be affected in a number of ways. The effects of VR may change the way young minds work in ways that we do not yet understand.

So, while there are concerns about how much screen time children can have when using virtual reality devices, not many studies have been done on this topic. It's speculated that children who spend too much time in front of screens will become more susceptible to eye problems like headaches and dry eyes. But this is only a minor concern in the grand scheme of things. If the current generation fails to discern reality from the metaverse and vice versa, we could have a whole new pandemic on our hands.

Thoughts on the Future

As scary as all that sounds, there are many positives to the metaverse and creating a virtual world for the masses. We've already discussed the medical possibilities attached to VR, not to mention what the metaverse could end up doing for the job market. The question, then, is "What's next?"

Technology is evolving at an exponential rate. And because the future of technology is always changing and advancing, it's hard to say just how it will change in the future. But there are some interesting predictions. For instance, many experts predict that humans will merge with machines and become part of the technological infrastructure. This could lead to a world where people are so interconnected with technology that they can't function without it. Moreover, it's said that the vast majority of the population will be cybernetic. And the few who aren't will be unable to communicate with the rest of society.

> *What we can say with near certainty is that virtual reality is here to stay.*

And lest we forget, Elon Musk himself—who at one time was famously against the rise of AI—recently implanted a chip in a pig's brain. Keep in mind that his goal is to achieve this in humans and on a mass scale. The man who took over Tesla also currently has the "TeslaBot" in the works. According to Musk, he hopes this android will have multi-faceted benefits, such as taking the place

225

of laborers or serving as a friend. Combined with the metaverse, our world could look radically different than how we presently know it.2

If that wasn't scary enough, another prediction is that we'll live forever because our minds will be uploaded into a computer and our consciousness will live in a virtual reality world, possibly the metaverse. These predictions may sound strange, but they're based on data from what has already happened with technology so far. Who knows what the future holds?

What we can say with near certainty is that virtual reality is here to stay. And VR is only just beginning to hit the mainstream market. As it becomes more popular, people are predicting that it will be used for everything from recreation to therapy. Experts project that VR will continue to grow and change with society as new uses are found for the technology. For example, one game developer predicts that VR will eventually become so advanced that users will be able to feel things like raindrops.

And this kind of innovation is only the beginning. We already talked about developers working on gloves that provide tactile feedback through haptic technology. When you're immersed in a virtual world, it's still fairly easy to tell what's real and what's a simulation. But as the technology advances and allows for more lifelike experiences, there may come a day when you can't tell one from the other.

As we discussed a few chapters back, blockchain technology is predicted to completely transform the way we do business. It has the potential to eliminate fraud, improve supply chains, and increase cybersecurity. It's important to understand that blockchain technology isn't just about cryptocurrency. In fact, the blockchain is used for much more than just digital currency. It can be used in many different industries like finance, energy, healthcare, and more. Basically, any industry where information is transferred or sold can benefit from this technology.

It's predicted that blockchain will change not only how we interact with businesses but also how we interact with each other. It will make it easier to verify authenticity of products or services and create a paperless system that will help prevent fraud. And given the roles that crypto and the blockchain play in the metaverse, we could be on the cusp of a complete monetary reset. But rather than restart our existing currency, we will be ditching it in favor of digital money.

In the future, experts believe there will be no such thing as a 9 to 5 job. Instead, our work will be divided into three different types of work: Creative work, which is focused on innovation and creativity; Socializing work, which is focused on empathy and relationships; and Transactional work, which includes tasks like data entry.

As the world continues to become more technologically advanced, it's inevitable that some jobs will disappear or change drastically. In a future where robots do most of our transactional tasks and AI helps us with creative tasks, socializing work seems to be the main focus for humans in the workplace. However, these changes also seem to create space for new professions that we can't even imagine yet. If there's one thing that is almost certain to be borne from the metaverse, it's jobs. For the first time in history, there will be an all-new marketplace that requires professions from all around the world. And as stated, some professions that are ultimately found in the metaverse may not even exist yet.

So, we'll just have to wait and see what unfolds like everyone else. The metaverse is coming faster than we think. And when it arrives, it will change the way we live, work, play, and possibly even love. The experts have already begun to weigh in on what they think will happen in the future. But how the future ultimately unfolds will be up to us. Can we make the most of the metaverse and use it as a source of good for society? Or, like we did with the internet, will we turn it into a toxic wasteland of blind insults and cancel culture?

Conclusion

It's important to consider the ramifications, if any, of using the metaverse. We've already discussed the possible struggles some people might have with this new way of life, but what about the long-term effects on our society as a whole? Will users who have been exposed to the metaverse for extended periods of time have a hard time going back to normal, everyday life?

If current trends are any indication, this is likely going to be the case with the metaverse. Many youths struggle with attention-based issues due to constant exposure to smartphones and video games. It's only natural to assume that these effects would only be amplified in a VR world. But it's not just children who should be concerned. In light of the pandemic and the public's shift to remote work, it's getting harder for many adults to get back into the groove of the life they used to live.

Whether it's returning to the office or just going to the store, prolonged exposure to digital worlds, whether they're advanced or not, tend to make life in the real world more challenging. Many studies and research are needed before we'll know for sure if the metaverse has more risk than reward. And that's what has many people afraid for the future.

Enjoy this Excerpt From
Big Things Have Small Beginnings

Read more books in the Motivation, Business & Leadership series. In this excerpt, Wes Berry shares insights from his decades in business, drawing from great leaders throughout history to guide you in learning the same strategies and tactics that made them successful; an understanding that will empower you to achieve success in both business and in life.

Chapter 1—Ambition…

For Better, or Worse?

Let's begin our discussion with "Ambition." Nothing in business will get accomplished without it. You simply can't play in the great game without ambition.

Ambition is an absolute essential. But make no mistake, for better or worse, genuine ambition involves struggle. We set out to achieve something that we believe is really worthwhile. And it is the achievement of that worthwhile goal that brings us a genuine sense of our own worth. We make a difference. We earn our dignity. But let me add that the very struggle itself, even in the absence of the success we set out to achieve, brings much of the same benefit to us. It makes us people with a purpose.

Ambition also puts considerable demands on us. It requires a whole lot more of us than just our lofty "ambitions," our dreams in life. It requires a toughness of mind and spirit that only really grows in us once we enter the ring, once we begin to play in the great game. And success is guaranteed to no one.

But if you're not willing to lose, you shouldn't be playing the game.

What is ambition?

For most people the term is a little ambiguous, isn't it? You're sitting at your desk shootin' the breeze over morning coffee with a co-worker, and your department head walks by.

"She's ambitious," you say.

Is it a compliment? Or is it a castigation? The answer to that question depends largely on whether or not you consider yourself to be ambitious, and for what reason—that is, to what end. And be assured that this discussion is not a new one.

Seventeenth-century philosopher, statesman, and jurist Sir Francis Bacon pondered this same point in his essay On Ambition (1612). In his now-archaic English, he writes:

So ambitious men, if they find the way open for their rising, and still get forward, they are rather busy than dangerous;

but if they be checked in their desires, they become secretly discontent, and look upon men and matters with an evil eye, and are best pleased, when things go backward; which is the worst property in a servant of a prince, or state.

Well isn't that clear as a bell? But, in fact, it sure does ring true!

He's saying that when ambitious men are allowed to engage in their passion, they become marvelously busy and industrious. They get stuff done! Contrary to common suspicion, he says, they do not become dangerous. On the contrary, he adds, the danger of ambition usually arises when such men are denied the pursuit of their ambitions, and then become a veritable danger to society, primarily out of the frustration and the consequent bitterness that follows. Rather than steering their formidable energies toward the good of society, they instead channel them toward its damage and destruction. This, of course, is particularly onerous when such frustrated men are servants of a prince, or of a state. Cautiously, Bacon instructs princes to manage ambitious people and channel their activities such that their creativity and ambitions are given breath, if not even wings.

Therefore it is good for princes, if they use ambitious men, to handle it, so as they be still progressive and not retrograde; which, because it cannot be without inconvenience, it is good not to use such natures at all.

In the plain English of today, he's suggesting that, if ambitious—and therefore productive—people cannot have their ambitions nurtured by the activities for which they have been enlisted, then it would be much better never to have enlisted such people at all, so that their frustrated ambition doesn't end up frustrating the success of a venture.

More than a few business writers have drawn parallels between the characteristics required for success in business with those required for success in war. With certain obvious limitations, it makes sense. The challenge, in both war and in business, of pitting oneself against fierce competitors, merely scratches the surface.

Bacon addresses this as well, but points out that an overly ambitious man may crave the accolades of greatness more than the doing of the great thing for the right reasons. He might report success where none existed solely for his own advancement.

An overly ambitious military officer might look forward to chaos. Chaos might well be his opportunity for advancement! He would crave the opportunities that battle presents. He might even wager selfishly with the lives under his command.

And then, if his misguided ambition really grabs a hold of him to where he starts to lose control, being acutely aware of the opportunity that chaos could bring, such a man might go so far as to create the chaos himself, regardless of the wisdom of his battlefield decisions, and particularly regardless of the sacrifice of the lives of his soldiers. As his opportunity lies in chaos, he could look to create such an environment for his own advantage.

And ambitious people know well the maxim, "The greater the risk, the greater the rewards." If successful, therefore, making risky wagers might seem the thing to do. Taken to the extreme, advancement by assassination might even be within the character of this type of individual. Hmmm, talk about ambition gone awry, right?

There's little doubt but that an openly ambitious man in the military is a recipe for disaster. As such, these very ambitions will block the achievements that an ambitious man strives for. Is it any wonder that highly ambitious individuals are almost chronically beset with dissatisfaction? In a military structure, this trait could lead to real complications.

Balance

The trick is to have just the right amount of ambition. The "Goldilocks" zone of ambition is ideal for a military career. Too little ambition and nothing gets done; too much and you are constantly discontent, leading to unwise or dangerous actions that could prove disastrous. Just the right measure of modest ambition, and you've got the perfect recipe for a truly effective and trusted officer.

The great Chinese General and war strategist, Sun Tzu, victorious in battle after battle back in the 6th century BC, elaborated on this quandary with his The Art of War, certainly one of the greatest books ever written. Even today, it is studied in virtually all military academies. And now the business world has grown well aware of the application of Sun Tzu's war principles and practices to the current art of business.

As the great general says, "In the midst of chaos, there is also opportunity." And yet, while Sun Tzu recognized the impact of this principle, he also clearly cautioned military leaders to maintain a discerning eye over an overtly ambitious man, one who could abuse a chaotic condition to advance his personal glory rather than for true battlefield success.

I've got to agree with Sun Tzu. It is entirely true that some are simply too ambitious to serve in the military. I'd rather say that some are not meant for a peacetime military; although I would prefer to say that some have an affinity for audacity, a willingness to take surprisingly bold risks. In the words of Fredrick the Great "L'audace, l'audace, toujours l'audace," or, as translated and requoted by WWII's outstandingly-successful war leader General George Patton, "Audacity, audacity, always audacity!"

Let's face it. Ambition is a powerful sword, and appreciably so when it's wielded by a person of integrity. When it is associated with a few individuals who are unafraid to openly strive for success, the results can be substantial.

Timing

There is one key factor which may be largely out of your hands: timing. Perhaps it is all about timing—when you are born and when you come of age. If the skills and traits you possess are in need, and your course is set to take the greatest advantage, then you can achieve what you were born to be.

Don't get me wrong. I'm not talking about little things here. If you believe you are meant for greatness, and refuse to let failures distract you, then you can achieve great things. And these great things will advance not only yourself, but those around you. In fact, with an additional touch of good fortune, you may well end up advancing Society or Mankind itself primarily as a result of your intrepid audacity!

When an outlier happens to possess the physical and mental strengths required, and has the audacity to act boldly with his or her ambitions, in the right place at the right time…well…this is the making of a Caesar. And it was owing to the ambition of a Caesar that the greatness of Rome was born.

Julius Caesar

Greatness? You bet. It was none other than Julius Caesar (100-44BC), and his immediate successors Augustus (63BC-14AD) and Tiberius (42BC-37AD), who converted the early Republic of Rome into the mighty Roman Empire, ushering in the Pax Romana (Latin for "Roman Peace"), a period of relative peace and prosperity that lasted throughout the known world of that time for over 200 years. To date, this is the longest period of widespread general peace the world has ever known.

Look at the words spoken by Shakespeare's Marc Antony (83-30BC), a Roman general and statesman who also played a significant role in the birth of the Empire, words chosen partly to eulogize his admired friend Julius Caesar following Caesar's assassination by another once-close associate, Brutus:

The noble Brutus hath told you Caesar was ambitious: If it were so, it was a grievous fault; And grievously hath Caesar answer'd it... Come I to speak at Caesar's funeral. He was my friend, faithful and just to me: But Brutus says he was ambitious; And Brutus is an honorable man.

Yes, Caesar was ambitious for himself, but also for his friends and for Rome. You might ask how this can be, for ambition is thought of as greed. I tell you ambition, greed, and all the baser forms—thought of as the darker side of human nature—are simply tools. Like a gun. In the hands of a criminal, a gun affects society with pain. But, that same gun in the hand of the hero protects the innocent, and enforces the security that society requires to conduct the gentrification of its citizens.

Caesar's identity was Rome, and so his ambition was for Rome. What greater gift than audacious ambition for the citizens of Rome? And even in death did his efforts continue to work to unify Rome. To be sure, his legacy took about 80 years to usher in the Pax Romana; but many have argued persuasively that it was, in fact, Julius Caesar's death that began the long-term unification of Rome.

Granted, much blood was spilled for Rome to be Rome, and, true, justice and security were reserved mostly to those who were Roman citizens. Still, in the provinces it was better than it had been. The fall of Rome just before 400AD began the onset of the Dark Ages, and the consequent loss of the amazing peace, stability, and protection of its citizenry that were such hallmarks of the Empire. The eventual downfall of the Roman Empire was clearly a great loss to all mankind. And it would be another 500-1,000 years before the Dark Ages would finally come to a close, and the world could again pick itself up and begin to shine a little brighter light on itself.

So was Caesar an ambitious man? I'm sure he was. It's certainly fair to say that Caesar played at the very top of the great game. And all mankind should thank him for his ambition. He had the audacity to be ambitious, and the mindfulness to use these traits to impose his willfulness to unite his countrymen.

Was he perfect? Hardly. But, even with all his faults, and all of Rome's faults and limitations, the ambition and greed of Rome evolved into the audacity to force the peace. Yes, the desire of greed enforced the peace.

How, you might ask, can this be? Simple. Peace was the ambition of Caesar, and it was the ultimate ambition of Rome. Because with security comes prosperity, and the greed of Rome created prosperity. Sure, it was imperfect, as all institutions made by man inevitably are plagued with imperfections. However, with Rome, life was grander and better than what the world was without it. Rome changed the world from one of relentless tribal barbarism to one of organized, cooperative civilization. The societal revolution it ushered in, made possible by the force of the Pax Romana, brought advancements to the civilization of humankind that are practicably impossible to sketch out in full.

Keep in mind, the goal of every military commander is victory, and with victory there is peace.

So in *"Understanding Ambitious People,"* it's important to consider the necessary circumstances of the times in which you deal. But, as we've said, ambition is a powerful force. Therefore, in the absence of the engagement of war, it is clear that soldiers—those ambitious souls biting at the bit for action—must be kept busy, even when little of crucial importance is to be done. In days of old, the Army, in times of peace, would often be put to building roads, bridges, and other such useful tasks. Okay. Not bad. Not war, to be sure. But a pretty useful and practical means to occupy those ambitious soldiers in a constructive pursuit.

Need we look very far to see the effects of our not heeding these principles today?

How about all those dedicated, self-sacrificing—read "ambitious for peace and freedom"—soldiers in Iraq and Afghanistan who fought beside our own American troops to secure some measure of peace, tranquility, and future prosperity for their own families and countrymen following the close of the Iraq war? We overlooked these ambitious men who, in defeat, were left without a means to fulfill their ambitions. These soldiers, trained in the arts of war, were left without a feeling of usefulness. Is it any wonder they became an insurgent force? Is it any wonder that they took out their frustrations using the skills they had acquired? Is it really any wonder they set about inflicting so much disruption to what should have been a lasting peace?

Perhaps the peace could have been maintained, however, if these men could have had their ambition channeled into tasks, albeit challenging, that they themselves could see as moving them in the direction of that lasting peace. Even a fool's errand would have avoided the damage that they inflicted on that troubled land.

If you're worried about your own ambition, pause a minute. Especially if you're worried about risk and about failure...well, then join the group. We all face it. If you're concerned that maybe you just don't have the critical leadership traits to be successful in the great game, maybe you're right—for now. But I'm here to tell you that all of what you need can be learned. It's the learning, the relentless attention to the small beginnings that will make all the difference. And those small things are often incredibly challenging.

Take some encouragement from the words of President Teddy Roosevelt. In his speech at the Sorbonne in Paris (April 23, 1910), he famously proclaimed:

> *It is not the critic who counts; not the man who points out how the strong man stumbles, or where the doer of deeds could have done them better. The credit belongs to the man who is actually in the arena, whose face is marred by dust and sweat and blood; who strives valiantly; . . . who at best*

knows in the end the triumph of high achievement, and who at worst, if he fails, at least fails while daring greatly.

For Julius Caesar, the moment of decision probably came on January 10, 49BC at the river Rubicon, the boundary line between Gaul and the Roman Republic. By crossing this minor river, everyone knew, Caesar was leading his legions into a civil war in his beloved Rome. He uttered the famous phrase "alea iacta est ("the die has been cast"). And today, the phrase "crossing the Rubicon" has since come to mean passing "the point of no return." At that moment he knew that he was risking it all on a roll of the dice.

A Word About Risk

So, what drives a person to take such a monumental risk? What type of ambition must a man have to put his very life, and all that he has achieved in that life to date, on the line? For Caesar, it's pretty clear that his ambition on that fateful day was fueled, at the very least, by his ambition to reform the city he loved. He clearly believed he could govern more wisely than the current government, and history has borne out that wisdom. Did he have personal ambitions for his own greatness? For his own place in the history of the world? I suppose he did. In fact, I can't imagine that he did not, at least in some way. But where does that come from?

243

I'd say it comes from a mountain of self-knowledge, a ton of self-confidence, and years of challenging oneself to develop the skills necessary to carry out that ambition.

At that point, it might be better said that, given what he saw before him in Rome, and given who he had become himself, it might have been more unthinkable for him to have suppressed that ambition to reform his Rome. As you can see, ambition can require a willingness to roll the dice, especially if you have a notion that those dice just might be loaded in your favor.

There's always a chance you'll fall flat on your face. There's always that chance that you'll embarrass yourself, that you'll end up spending countless hours and every dime you can beg, borrow, or steal to fulfill that relentless ambition of yours. And there's always that chance that it'll bring you to abject failure, to the loss of your former financial stability, maybe even to the tragic loss of your friends, and heaven forbid, even your family. Yes, you could fail.

But here's the rub: If you're not willing to lose, you're not allowed to play in the game.

There is no one alive who has been successful who did not have failures! So, at least to start, you're in pretty good company. BUT, the critical lesson here is that people who were successful learned from those same failures. So very often it was those classrooms of failure that, once their powerful lessons were learned, led to their success. They had learned to play in the great game.

With every opportunity, there is also risk. And with risk, by definition, there is always the possibility of loss. It takes guts to wrap ourselves around that.

But here's the good news. For all practical purposes, there is no risk that is insurmountable. And the immense depth of satisfaction you receive is often equal to the amount of risk you take.

Lets face it. If success was devoid of risk, if success took us down a path of ease and comfort, well then everybody else would be there too!

There's no question that I'm thankful to God for the wonderful blessings I've enjoyed. But when I say that, I'm saying that I'm thankful for stuff that He's given me that I know He's also given to just about everyone else on the planet too. And, as we'll see in our next chapter, He's especially given a whole bunch of great stuff to anyone who's living in this rather amazing capitalist democracy we call the United States of America.

America – the Land of Ambitious People

If you're looking to start and run a business—large or small—there is simply nowhere else on earth that you will have the same advantages and opportunities as you will in this country of ours.

Let me flesh that out a little bit.

It might be reasonably argued that throughout our history America has been the most "ambitious" country in the world.

I know what you're thinking. Hmmm, that word "ambition." As I mentioned earlier, for some people it puts a lousy taste in their mouth. We've all known people who are so ambitious that they think nothing of stepping on whomever and whatever they need to just so they can get what they want. Some politicians come to mind, right? How about a couple of your favorite dictators? Hitler was a pretty ambitious guy, don't you think? Yeah, and that makes him pretty loathsome, right?

But wait a minute. If ambition in its purest form is "an eager or strong desire to achieve something," (thank you, Daniel Webster!), then maybe we ought to be looking at a few other models of ambition too...you know, just to be fair to the word and maybe round this thing out.

George Washington had a pretty strong ambition to establish the world's very first government by and for its people. And he and his Founding Father compatriots exercised that ambition at the very risk of their respectable fortunes, their personal comfort, and ultimately at the risk of their lives. Abraham Lincoln had an unbelievably strong ambition to unite a divided country even while eradicating its widespread practice of slavery, upon which half the country's economy heavily rested.

And how about Henry Ford? When you get a chance, take a closer look at the risks that guy took! The obstacles that fell across his path! That was some remarkable ambition, to say the very least.

It's certainly fair to say that astronauts are ambitious too. Like Kirk, they want to "boldly go where no one has gone before." How about doctors? How else could anybody endure that much concentrated education—let alone ridiculously high insurance premiums—without a couple bucketsful of ambition ?

Ambition is like money. It in itself is pretty neutral. It's up to us to use it to do good…or not. But you know what? If you really have a desire to succeed in your business, it is absolutely going to take ambition—that is, the really good kind.

Let's be clear here: your very desire to succeed IS your ambition. Embrace it! Without ambition, your chances of success in business are pretty slim.

As we've seen in this chapter, ambition is what gives us the people who move our world forward. It's behind our Julius Caesars, our Franklin D. Roosevelts, and it's even behind every runner who ever set out one day to finally train for and complete that elusive 26-mile, 385-yard marathon.

And the absence of ambition? Well, we've all known our share of couch potatoes, haven't we?

In conclusion, know this: truly ambitious people would rather taste defeat than never have the chance to wear the laurel wreaths of victory. And the best ambitions are not just for oneself, but for an ideal, something greater than the individual.

To read more, you can get the book at

www.WesBerryGroup.Com.

References

Introduction

1. "More than 12m players watch Travis Scott concert in Fortnite." The Guardian.
https://www.theguardian.com/games/2020/apr/24/travis-scott-concert-fortnite-more-than-12m-players-watch

Chapter 1: The New Internet

1. "11 Big Changes to the Internet from the Past Decade."
Entrepreneur. https://www.entrepreneur.com/article/279844

2. "Facebook is spending at least $10 billion this year on its metaverse division." The Verge.
https://www.theverge.com/2021/10/25/22745381/facebook-reality-labs-10-billion-metaverse

3. "Who Invented the Internet?" History.
https://www.history.com/news/who-invented-the-internet

4. "Global digital population as of January 2021." Statista. https://www.statista.com/statistics/617136/digital-population-worldwide/

Chapter 2: What Is the Metaverse?

1. "The History of Facebook and How It Was Invented." ThoughtCo. https://www.thoughtco.com/who-invented-facebook-1991791

2. "Mark in the Metaverse." The Verge. https://www.theverge.com/22588022/mark-zuckerberg-facebook-ceo-metaverse-interview

3. "Everything You Need to Know About the Oculus Quest & Oculus Quest 2." Program-Ace. https://program-ace.com/blog/oculus-quest/

4. "The Ultimate Guide to Augmented Reality," HubSpot. https://blog.hubspot.com/marketing/augmented-reality-ar

Chapter 5: Crypto In the Metaverse

1. A little-known cryptocurrency spiked 400% after Facebook changed its name to Meta - CNBC
https://www.cnbc.com/2021/11/01/decentraland-mana-cryptocurrency-rallies-after-facebook-name-change.html?utm_term=Autofeed&utm_medium=Social&utm_content=Main&utm_source=Twitter#Echobox=1635781012

2. Are NFTs The New Crypto? A Guide To Understanding Non-Fungible Tokens - *Forbes*
https://www.google.co.in/amp/s/www.forbes.com/sites/forbesbusinesscouncil/2021/06/09/are-nfts-the-new-crypto-a-guide-to-understanding-non-fungible-tokens/amp/
https://www.wundermanthompson.com/insight/governments-in-the-metaverse

Chapter 6: From the Silver Screen to Your VR Headset

1. "Ready Player One (film)." Wikipedia.
https://en.wikipedia.org/wiki/Ready_Player_One_(film)

2. "Applications of Virtual Reality in Medicine." News Medical Life Sciences. https://www.news-medical.net/health/Applications-of-Virtual-Reality-in-Medicine.aspx

3. "Creating Full Sensory Experiences: The Future of AR/VR/MR/XR." Radiant Vision Systems. https://www.radiantvisionsystems.com/blog/creating-full-sensory-experiences-future-ar/vr/mr/xr

Chapter 7: The Sims in Your Living Room

1. "History Of The Sims: How A Major Franchise Evolved From City-Builder To Life-Simulator." GameSpot. https://www.gamespot.com/gallery/history-of-the-sims-how-a-major-franchise-evolved-/2900-1623/

2. "The Top 50 Best-Selling Video Games of All Time." HP. https://www.hp.com/us-en/shop/tech-takes/top-50-best-selling-video-games-all-time

3. "5 Recent Infamous Website Crashes." CDNIFY. https://cdnify.com/blog/5-recent-infamous-website-crashes/

Chapter 8: The Applications of Metaverse, So Far

1. "Making Reality Virtual: How VR "Tricks" Your Brain." Frontiers for Young Minds. https://kids.frontiersin.org/articles/10.3389/frym.2018.00062

2. "Education Applications of The Metaverse." PubMed.gov https://pubmed.ncbi.nlm.nih.gov/34897242/

3. "Applications of Virtual Reality in Medicine." News Medical Life Sciences. https://www.news-medical.net/health/Applications-of-Virtual-Reality-in-Medicine.aspx

4. Understanding The Metaverse Through Real-World Examples - Influencer Marketing Hub: https://influencermarketinghub.com/metaverse-examples/

Chapter 10: Choose Your Avatar

1. Stefan Cook Enters The Metaverse With A Collection For The Sims - *Vogue*: https://www.vogue.com/article/stefan-cooke-the-sims

2. Beauty In The Metaverse: Where It's Heading? - Vogue Business.

https://www.voguebusiness.com/beauty/beauty-in-the-metaverse-where-its-heading

Chapter 12: Get Fit in the Metaverse

1. "This extremely slippery VR treadmill could be your next home gym." The
Verge. https://www.theverge.com/2020/10/7/21504797/virtuix-omni-one-vr-treadmill-announce-crowdfunding

2. Could Fitness Be The Killer App In The Metaverse? Or Is It Gaming? Or Both? -
Forbes: https://www.forbes.com/sites/timbajarin/2021/12/24/could-fitness-be-the-killer-app-for-the-metaverse-or-is-it-gaming-or-both/?sh=2843d213146f

3. Virtual Workouts, Real Sweat -
Mint: https://www.livemint.com/technology/virtual-workouts-real-sweat-exercising-in-the-metaverse-with-the-meta-quest-2-11643553808548.html

4. How To Get Fit In The Metaverse -
Techrader: https://www.techradar.com/in/how-to/how-to-get-fit-in-the-metaverse

Chapter 13: Dating In the Metaverse

1. Dating In The Metaverse? - South China Morning
Post: https://www.scmp.com/lifestyle/family-
relationships/article/3165692/dating-metaverse-you-need-some-
ground-rules-avoid

Chapter 14: Is the Metaverse Necessary?

1. Mark Zuckerberg on Why Facebook Is Rebranding to Meta –
The Verge. https://www.theverge.com/22749919/mark-
zuckerberg-facebook-meta-company-rebrand

Chapter 15: A Safer World For Everyone

1. Founder of Austin's Bumble testifies in favor of digital sexual
harassment bill. - Austin American – Statesman.
https://www.statesman.com/story/news/politics/state/2019/03/25/
founder-of-austins-bumble-testifies-in-favor-of-digital-sexual-
harassment-bill/5619653007/

2. Video Games and Chats are Hunting Groups for Sexual
Predators. *The New York Times* -

https://www.nytimes.com/interactive/2019/12/07/us/video-games-child-sex-abuse.html

Chapter 16: Life After Metaverse

1. Elon Musk's Neuralink Puts Computer Chips In Pigs' Brains In Bid To Cure Diseases - NBC News: https://www.nbcnews.com/tech/tech-news/elon-musk-s-neuralink-puts-computer-chips-pigs-brains-bid-n1238782

2. Elon Musk Builds a Machine to Download our Personalities. The Street - https://www.thestreet.com/technology/elon-musk-builds-a-machine-to-download-our-brain-and-personalities

About The Author

Wesley Berry is the host of *The People's Voice,* a weekly radio talk show on WDTK Detroit's "The Patriot" 1400AM & 101.5FM Sundays at noon. The show's format features both controversial and unifying topics.

As Wesley himself says it, "As the show's host, I'm being guided by the principle that reasonable people can disagree without being disagreeable. Polite discourse of controversial subjects is fundamental to a civil society, and *The People's Voice* is committed to providing a forum where opposing views can be respectfully exchanged." You're always invited to review the past radio episodes at **www.wesberrygroup.com**.

Through the years, he's provided consulting services to over forty businesses, even while simultaneously establishing a retail franchise system that operated thirty units in five States. Additionally, he's served as Headmaster of a State-Licensed Private Vocational School, and as a licensed real estate agent, having participated in over thirty commercial transactions.

As an entrepreneur, Wes demonstrated a strategic style of management by building a multi-million dollar brick-and-mortar business. In 1995, his business expanded to the clicks of the Internet, causing him to adjust and sharpen his marketing skills to where they soon proved exceptionally well-suited to the new and radically different online arena. He operated under several brands, including Flower Delivery Express, a $60M world-class business servicing millions of customers in over 150 countries. After a 40-year business career, he divested himself of all business interests in 2016 and retired.

Wes has collaborated on designing sets for both ABC and CBS television shows, has appeared as a guest on several talk shows, and has been interviewed countless times by broadcast and print media. His many media appearances include: *NPR, The Wall Street Journal, The London Times, Entrepreneur* and *Time* magazines, Fox News, Neil Cavuto, Geraldo Rivera, and John Stossel, to name a just few.

Major Honors and Awards:

- (O-5) by Michigan Governor Schneider

Wes has held memberships in: The Detroit Economic Club, Adcraft Club of Detroit, Rotary International, Optimists International, NAACP, Shriners International, Wabeek Country Club, Detroit Athletic Club, Detroit Gun Club, NRA, and at Kirk in the Hills Presbyterian Church, where he's taught Sunday School, ushered, and served on its Board of Trustees. He has also served on the Boards of an Educational Foundation, Community Youth Assistance, and Henry Ford Hospital.

- Major Honors and Awards:

- 2000 - Rotary International Paul Harris Fellow

- 2003 - Pheasant Ring Autistic Community Ring of Hope Community Service Award

- 2008 - NAACP Oakland County Chapter's Corporate Leadership Award

- 2008 - *Florist Review* magazine's Retail Florist of the Year for Community Involvement

- 2008 - Chamber of Commerce honoree as Business Person of the Year

- 2011 - Inc. magazine's Top 500|5000-ranked Fastest Growing Retailer

- 2012 - Optimist International's Business Person of the Year, Michigan District

- 2014 - Civil rights organization United We Walk's Community Leader Award

- 2016 - Commissioned Honorary Naval Commander (O-5) by Michigan Governor Schneider

- 2018 - Amazon #1 Best Selling Author, #1 Hot New Release, and International Best Seller

- 2019 - Business Insider, Books to Help You Build Wealth and Get More Done

- 2019 - New York Book Festival, Winner Best Business Book

- 2019 - Barnes & Noble's Top 5 Best Sellers of All Books Worldwide

- 2019 - *USA TODAY* Bestselling Author

- 2019 - *Wall Street Journal* Bestselling Author

- 2020 – National Speakers Association

Wes is a Freemason and currently serves as a Trustee of the Michigan Masonic Charitable Foundation. He also volunteers with a community group that provides wheelchair ramps to those in need. He's a graduate of Oakland Technical Center, having completed their Floriculture & Agriscience Program.

A dog lover, Wes enjoys fishing, and is constantly humbled by his golf game. He and his wife Mia have four sons and have been married for thirty years. They reside in West Bloomfield, Michigan.